Chess Mazes

A New Kind of
Chess Puzzle for Everyone

Bruce Alberston

2004
Russell Enterprises, Inc.
Milford, CT USA

Chess Mazes

ISBN: 1-888690-23-2

Published by:
Russell Enterprises, Inc.
P.O. Box 5460
Milford, CT 06460 USA

http://www.chesscafe.com
info@chesscafe.com

Cover design by Janel Lowrance

Printed in the United States of America

Table of Contents

Foreword

Amazing Mazes

According to conventional wisdom, if you want to become a better, stronger chessplayer, you should try to (1) increase your tactical ability; (2) learn how to think over the board; and (3) improve your chess vision. But it is not always quite that simple. Some of the best executed plans are ruined by simple blunders. And if you are one who often loses games by hanging pieces or missing mates, then this is the book for you.

There are many good books which present chess combinations and explain tactical motifs with the goal of training your tactical ability. Thinking techniques are also well covered in the game's literature. But what about visualization? This is where it is much more difficult to find good material. But now, Bruce Alberston's highly original work fills this gap.

To master his puzzles, you have to exert better control and command of the full potential of all the pieces and you have to visualize their movements in your mind's eye. This sounds more difficult than it is, but in fact only one piece moves in each maze. The result? Excellent training to avoid one-move blunders!

Another typical question concerning chess vision is: What is the minimum number of moves needed to get from one square to another? You will be challenged here as well, because the puzzles must be solved in the minimum number of moves.

I have only one caveat: don't forget that in a real game both players alternate moves, and so you must always watch out for your opponent's threats and plans.

I hope that you will enjoy winding your way through these mazes and improving your chess vision!

Karsten Müller
Hamburg, Germany
September 2004

Introduction

Chess Mazes is chess. The pieces are the same. They move and capture just the same. Check and checkmate are exactly the same. But there is one significant difference. The alternation of moves rule has been suspended. That means only one side gets to make moves. That side is White. Poor Black never gets to make any moves. All he can do it sit back and watch.

As a chess teacher I've tried out various techniques to develop visualization and planning skills for my students. The ideal planning situation is where one side gets to make a plan and carry it through without hindrance or interference from the opponent. How do you do that? Don't let him move.

That's how *Chess Mazes* was born. And without realizing it at the time, I had also invented a new kind of chess puzzle.

To do chess mazes it's assumed that you know:

(1) How the pieces move,
(2) Rules for check and checkmate,
(3) Chess notation.

If you are not familiar with chess notation, don't worry. You can easily figure out how to decipher it from the examples given. So let's get down to rules. We'll take *bishop mazes* as the sample. This is appropriate since the first maze I ever composed was a bishop maze.

Rules for Bishop Mazes (and Rook and Knight)

Rule Number One: You are White and your *maze piece* is the bishop. You can move that bishop around the board at will or almost at will. The one restriction is Rule Four. Only the white bishop is allowed to move.

Rule Number Two: Black gets a king and some pieces, the number of which will vary from position to position. However, none of the black pieces, king included, is allowed to move. This makes Black a passive, stationary, observer. He gets to observe the white bishop as it moves around the board. The one exception is Rule Four.

Rule Number Three: The game ends when the bishop places the black king in check. That's it. Put the enemy king in danger, put him in check, and the maze is solved. Sound easy doesn't it?

Rule Number Four: You may not place your bishop (*maze piece*) on a square where it is subject to capture by a black unit. You do that, place your piece *en prise* (i.e., possible to be captured), then Black is allowed to move, take your piece and White loses. You have to start over.

Rule Number Five: We give only the shortest solution in the back of the book. If the maze can be solved in X number of moves and it took you X plus one, well, you sort of solved it, but not in the most efficient manner. You won't find your solution given.

Bishop Mazes in Action

Now that you know the rules for bishop mazes let's see how it works in practice. We begin with sample position number one.

#1

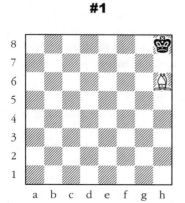

You know what you have to do — put the black king in check. The one move that you may not make is 1.Bh6-g7+.

#1a

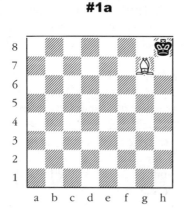

True, the black king is in check and it only took you one move to do it. But you've violated Rule Number Four — you put your bishop in danger, on a square where it can be captured. The black king can just take you off by

1...Kh8xg7. And that you cannot allow.

So, what can you do? It turns out that you have no less than five different ways to solve the maze. Here are the solutions:

1) 1.Bh6-g5 2. Bg5-f6+
2) 1.Bh6-f4 2. Bf4-e5+
3) 1.Bh6-e3 2. Be3-d4+
4) 1.Bh6-d2 2. Bd2-c3+
5) 1.Bh6-c1 2. Bc1-b2+

But a problem with five correct solutions is not much of a problem. What we're going to do is cut down your options, so there is really only one way (occasionally two) to solve the maze. If you have too many ways out, then it's not a very good maze. So, here is the same position with a slight adjustment.

#2

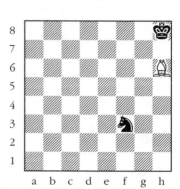

By adding the black knight on f3 we've created a whole series of mined squares where the bishop may not go to. We already know about g7, the black king guards it. And the knight takes away g5, d2, e5, and d4. There are other squares as well but we mention only the most critical. That leaves only one solution, namely **1.Bc1** and **2.Bb2+**.

I trust you found it. And what happens if you used, say, three moves: 1.Bf8 2.Ba3 3.Bb2+. Well, you're on your own in this case, because the only solution given is the one with the fewest number of moves, which in this instance is two. Try and get into the habit of doing things in the shortest possible way. Now let's look at position #3.

#3

You can also capture enemy pieces with your bishop. In fact it is necessary if they stand in your way.

Here, a quick glance at the position tells you that the check must come by taking the f6-pawn, which in turn is guarded by the f2-rook. Both of these

enemy units will have to be eliminated, first the rook and then the pawn. It's done by **1.Be3 2.Bxf2 3.Bb6 4.Bd8 5.Bxf6+.**

#3a

I hope you figured it out.

Solving Bishop Mazes

There are two ways to solve bishop mazes, working forward and working backward. In the forward approach the bishop lurches ahead one move at a time until something clicks. It works best when the bishop has only one safe square each move along the way. Then, just by stumbling forward you eventually stumble into the final check which solves the maze.

For optimal results the backward approach seems to work best. Certainly this emphasizes the planning aspect of bishop mazes.

Sample position 3, which we just did, shows the backward approach in action. We immediately established that the bishop has to give its check by taking the f6-pawn. And we also saw that the pawn is guarded by the f2-rook.

This means that the maze has to be worked in two stages, first capture the rook and then the pawn.

Capturing the rook is relatively easy using the most direct route over the e3-square. So stage one is **1.Be3** and **2.Bxf2**. The next stage is to figure out how to get from f2 to f6. The mined squares that the bishop must avoid are c3, d4, e5, g5, and h4.

That leaves b2, d8, and e7 as the squares that the bishop has to reach. The bishop can reach b2 by the convoluted route 3.Bg3 4.Bd6 5.Ba3 6.Bb2, and it can reach d8 by a more direct method, **3.Bb6 4.Bd8**. Prefer the direct method since it is also the shortest.

To get the full benefit from *Chess Mazes* I strongly urge you to solve the positions directly from the diagrams, without out the aid of arrows or lines or any other devices you may come up with. You can work the mazes in your head just by looking at the diagram position. This is the way to build your visualization skills.

If you are an incorrigible board setter-upper (there are such people – your author is one of them) then by all means set the diagram position up on your board. But don't touch the pieces! Solve the problems in your head.

The Rest of the Mazes

The rules for bishop, rook, and knight mazes are all the same. You'll find further examples in Chapter One. When we get to queen, pawn, and king mazes, some modification of rule three is necessary. Instead of check, you play for checkmate. The details with additional examples are explained in Chapter Two.

Application to Real Chess

The planning and visualization skills that come from working on chess mazes appear to me self-evident. There's no need for further elaboration. They translate directly to over-the-board chess and have countless other applications as well. They are universal skills.

So too is seeing what's right under your nose. Unfortunately, many average players have trouble noticing what's staring them directly in the face. How many times have we seen Mr. Average Player place a piece right in the path of an opposing unit where it can be captured for nothing? All too many times.

And we know from experience that not all such mistakes get punished. Often the opponent (another average player) does not see what's right under his own nose and fails to make the capture. But do that against an experienced player and he'll take your pieces every time.

That's the reason for rule four. Don't do that. Don't put your pieces *en prise*. Train your eyes to see what's immediately in front of them. See where the enemy forces are striking. Eliminate the silly *en prise* mistakes, and you are absolutely certain to move up a class or two. That's a guarantee.

What about rules one and two, where only White gets to do something and Black must sit back as a helpless spectator? Does this happen in real chess games?

Of course it does. It happens every time one side obtains a huge material or positional superiority. The side with the advantage gets to call all the shots, the side with the disadvantage can only stand by and hope his opponent does not know how to win.

So it come down to this — does the superior side know how to convert his superiority into a win? Let's see some examples from practical play.

Actual Play

Our next position is taken from an endgame played in the East-Penn Jersey Chess League, 1957-1958 season. White has an overwhelming material advantage, an extra queen.

White should win easily if he knows what do. The winning plan consists of three parts:

(1) Restrict the movement of Black king
(2) Advance the white king to its optimal attacking square (c6)
(3) Mate with the queen

In the game White displayed perfect knowledge of the technique required.

#4
White to Move

The first move was **1.Qb5**.

#4a
after 1.Qb5

A "cut-off move" which keeps the black king confined to the board's edge. In fact Black is quite helpless here. All he can do is shift his king back and forth between a8 and a7.

Meanwhile, the white king moves up to c6 in five moves: **2.Kg2 3.Kf3 4.Ke4 5.Kd5 6.Kc6.** At the end Black's king stands once again on a8, and White finishes off with **7.Qb7** mate.

In this example only White's moves prove relevant, Black's shuttling king moves count for nothing.

Here is another endgame example from East-Penn Jersey Chess League, fall 1957. Here White's advantage consists of only one extra pawn (at g6) but with correct play it's enough for victory.

#5

White to Move

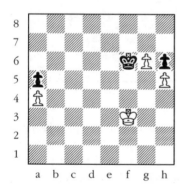

The first thing you notice is that the passed g-pawn restricts the movement of Black's king which may not play to the d-file or to the fifth rank. If he does this the g-pawn simply marches in to queen. That gives White a free hand for his king to go after the black a-pawn, win it, and promote his own a-pawn.

White's moves would be 1.Ke4 2.Kd4 3.Kc4 4.Kb5 and 5.Kxa5. There's nothing Black can do to stop it. His own king cannot leave the vicinity of the g6-pawn.

In the game White tried plan A, looking to win on the kingside where he has his extra pawn. The play went **1.Kf4 Kg7 2.Kf5 Kg8 3.Kf6 Kh8**, reaching this position:

#5a

White to Move

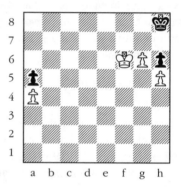

Here White paused to think. He saw that 4.Kf7 is a draw by stalemate, also that 4.g7+ Kg8 5.Kg6 comes to the same thing.

To his credit he switched to plan B and went after the a5-pawn by **4.Ke6 5.Kd6 6.Kc6 7.Kb5** and **8.Kxa5**. The opponent resigned after White got his new queen.

Again we see that only the moves of the winner carry any weight. He either knows how to win or he doesn't.

Finally we come to rule number five, where we emphasize that only the shortest and most efficient solution counts. Puttering around with your bishop does not count. Let's see why from our next example (this time not from the East-Penn Jersey Chess League).

#6
Black to Move

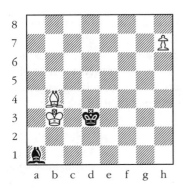

Clearly Black is aiming to make a draw. If he can eliminate the white h-pawn he has it, even if he loses his own bishop in the process. That's because White cannot checkmate with a lone king and bishop. It's just not possible to construct a mate with these few pieces. On the other hand if White succeeds in promoting his h-pawn, then he will win.

At the moment the black a1-bishop controls the queening square h8. But the bishop is about to be challenged for control of the long diagonal by White's threat, 1.Ba3 and 2.Bb2. That's bad news.

Moving the king, 1...Ke4, doesn't work in view of 2.Bc3, immediately wresting the diagonal from Black's hands. He has to move his bishop. But where?

Let's try 1...Bf6 2.Ba3 Ke4 3.Bb2

Kf5 4.Bxf6 Kg6 and we see that Black is one move too late, 5.h8=Q.

Perhaps now you've spotted where the black bishop must go. It can't just be any old square on the diagonal. There is precisely one square and the bishop must head there immediately.

That's **1...Bh8!**:

#6a

Now Black can deal with **2.Ba3 Ke4 3.Bb2 Kf5 4.Bxh8**.

#6b

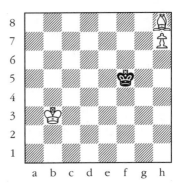

Because he has **4...Kg6 5.B-any Kxh7**. The h7-pawn is gone and Black makes his draw.

Precision in the selection of squares and accuracy in the timing of the moves — that's what rule number five is intended to get across.

The more efficient chess player is also the more successful chess player. He wins positions that might not otherwise be won, and he saves positions that otherwise would be lost. Develop your sense of timing and you're sure to increase your playing strength by a class or two. Another guarantee.

How else can *Chess Mazes* be used? Some students use mazes before the start of a tournament round. Working through a handful of mazes gets the mental juices flowing, so that when you sit down to play the game you're already in gear.

And you don't have to have any ulterior motive at all. You can chuck all the self-improvement reasons and just do mazes for the fun of it.

I certainly had fun composing *Chess Mazes*, and then had fun solving them. Fun is good.

Special thanks to Fred Wilson who suggested the title and who has also composed some wicked mazes in his time. Also, thanks to Hanon Russell and his crew for recognizing an original idea and putting it all together.

Bruce Alberston
Astoria, New York
September, 2004

Signs, Symbols

x	captures
+	check
!	a strong move
?	a weak move, an error
!?	a move worth consideration
?!	a dubious move
#	checkmate

Chapter One
Bishop, Rook, and Knight Mazes

These three pieces form a group since the rules for solving the mazes are essentially the same. Let's quickly recap the rules.

Rule Number One: White gets one kind of piece to work with, the *maze piece*. It will be either bishop, rook, or knight depending on the maze. Only White gets to make moves.

Rule Number Two: Black never gets to make a move. The one exception arises with Rule Number Four.

Rule Number Three: The maze is solved when White gives check to the black king.

Rule Number Four: White is not allowed to place his piece on a square where it can be captured. If he does that, places his piece *en prise*, Black is suddenly permitted to move and take the white piece.

Rule Number Five: Only the shortest solution counts.

Chess Mazes in Action

Here, we give several examples of the three types of mazes. Think of them as warm-ups for the main problems that follow.

A quick glance at the next position reveals that Black has all the checking squares covered save g2. So the task is to bring the bishop from a6 to g2 in the

shortest number of moves.

#7

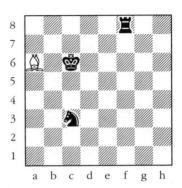

One way might be 1.Bd3 2.Bg6 3.Bh5 4.Bg4 5.Bh3 6.Bg2+. But it is not the shortest. That honor belongs to **1.Bc4 2.Be6 3.Bh3 and 4.Bg2+.**

#8

It's clear that the final move has to be **Bxd4+** But how does the bishop get to d4? There are several unguarded squares that line up with d4. These are a7 (after taking the pawn), g7, and g1. Examination reveals that it is not possible to reach a7 or g7 without putting the bishop *en prise*, so that leaves g1. And the solution is **1.Ba3 2.Be7 3.Bh4 4.Be1 5.Bxa5 6.Bc7 7.Bh2 8.Bg1 9.Bxd4+.**

#9

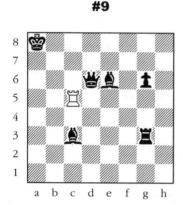

A rook maze. There are two unprotected squares where the rook might conceivably give check: e8 and a4. However, the one approach to e8, over the square e7, is guarded by the black queen. That means the rook must arrange to give its check at a4. It is done by **1.Rb5 2.Rb1 3.Rh1 4.Rh4 5.Ra4+.**

#10

Here it's clear that the one open square for the rook to give its check is at h1. How does the rook get there? By

1.Rb6 2.Rb3 3.Ra3 4.Ra8 5.Rg8 6.Rg1 7.Rh1+.

#11

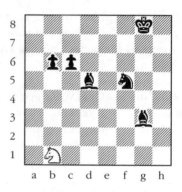

A knight maze. The black knight guards two checking squares, e7 and h6, which means that White must give his check at f6. The approach squares to f6 are the light squares d7, e8, g4 and h5. Only one of these is readily attainable. And the solution is **1.Nc3 2.Na4 3.Nxb6 4.Nd7 5.Nf6+.**

#12

Check has to be made on one of three light squares, e2, f3, or h3. This last square is unprotected, but to get to h3, the knight must first reach g5 or f4, and both these squares are guarded by black pieces. It's certain that White has

to go after the h5-bishop. After taking, one of the two squares, e2 or f3, will open up. So, **1.Na3 2.Nb5 3.Na7 4.Nc6 5.Ne7 6.Nf5 7.Ng3 8.Nxh5 9.Ng3 10.Ne2+.**

A player starts the game with 16 men: eight pieces, eight pawns. Normally each of the pieces and some of the pawns will have their say, but it's quite rare for one particular unit to suddenly hog the show. However, as the forces on both sides are whittled down through exchanges and the endgame approaches, then it may become possible for one piece to display a short burst of activity.

Diagram 13 is from Lasker vs. Rubinstein, St. Petersburg 1914, where four consecutive rook moves decided the contest. White has the advantage in operating space and this grants greater activity for his king and rook.

#13
White to Move

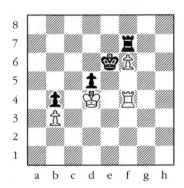

At the moment he is stymied on the kingside where Black has blockaded the f6-pawn. This prompts Lasker to seek greener pastures for his rook. That's the explanation for his next move.

1.Rf2, looking to become active on the queen-side. The first tactical point is that Black cannot take the f6-pawn without falling into a lost king and pawn ending. For example: 1...Rxf6 2.Rxf6+ Kxf6 3.Kxd5, and White comes back 4.Kc5, wins the b-pawn, 5.Kxb4, and the game.

Rubinstein temporizes, **1...Kd6,** and Lasker continues with his plan, **2.Ra2.** Again the f6-pawn is poisoned, 2...Rxf6 3.Ra6+ Ke7 4.Rxf6 Kxf6 5.Kxd5 etc. Rubinstein tries to make his own rook active, **2...Rc7,** when there follows **3.Ra6+ Kd7.** Now the hasty pawn grab 4.Kxd5 allows 4...Rc3, getting behind the white pawns and causing trouble.

But Lasker's next precise move quashed all resistance: **4.Rb6!** Black resigned, since 4...Rc3 now fails to 5.Rxb4 (this would be the fifth consecutive rook move had the game continued) 5...Rf3 6.Ke5 with 7.Rf4 coming up.

A more sustained series of rook moves occurs when one side continually offers his rook to make a draw.

#14
Black to Move

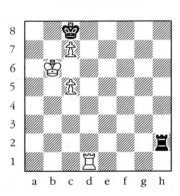

In diagram 14, it is obvious that Black is in bad shape. White is threatening nothing less than 1.Rd8 mate. Withdrawing the black rook to the home rank, 1...Rh8, doesn't help in view of 2.Rd8+ Rxd8 3.cxd8=Q+ Kxd8 4.Kb7, when White's remaining pawn has a clear path to the queening square c8. Something drastic is called for.

First, **1...Rb2+** to see where the white king goes; White derives no benefit from 2.Ka6 letting his c7-pawn go after 2...Kxc7. Black, though still a pawn down, should easily be able to make a draw. So, **2.Kc6** is pretty much forced, still threatening to mate at d8. Yet with the white king at c6, Black's king is stalemated, and all Black has to do to draw is dump his rook. This is done by **2...Rd2!**:

#14a

If White takes, 3.Rxd2, the resulting position is stalemate, a draw. White could try shifting to another file, **3.Rh1**, but again Black opposes him, **3...Rh2 4.Ra1 Ra2** and so forth, Black continually offering his rook along the second rank. There is nothing White can do about it. It's either a perpetual attack on the white rook or a draw by stale-

mate if White takes the black rook. And how many rook moves can both sides make before the draw is agreed? Don't ask.

In his examination of basic bishop and pawn endings in 1856, an Italian endgame composer named Luigi Centurini came up with a number of extended bishop maneuvers similar to what we here call mazes. Diagram 15 is one of his seven-movers.

#15
White to Play

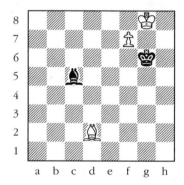

To start with, White has to chase the enemy bishop from the a3-f8 diagonal. That is done by bringing his own bishop to f8, **1.Bc3 Ba3 2.Bg7 Bb4 3.Bf8**.

Now the black bishop has to take up a new post along the f8-h6 diagonal, at g7 or h6. If 3...Bd2 4.Ba3 Bh6 5.Bb2, Black runs out of constructive moves. His king must give way, 5...Kf5, and that fails to 6.Bg7.

So he tries **3...Bc3 4.Ba3 Bg7 5.Bc1**, but once again Black runs out of moves, and **5...Kf6** is met by **6.Bb2+ Kg6 7.Bxg7** winning.

That same year, 1856, Centurini

14

topped himself with a sustained eleven-move bishop sequence.

#16
White to Move

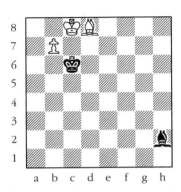

The ending is won if White can bring his bishop to the b8-h2 diagonal, challenging Black for control. That means the bishop must get to c7 or b8. At present Black is solidly guarding c7, so White tries to bring his bishop to b8. That will force the black king over to a6, momentarily weakening his protection of c7.

The initial moves are **1.Bh4 Kb6 2.Bf2+ Ka6**. Now comes the key move, **3.Bc5!**. Black is forced to make a move with his bishop, and this in turn will provide White with a vital tempo later on.

After **3...Bg3 4.Be7** White threatens 5.Bd8 and 6.Bc7, thus forcing the black king to abandon a6 and return to c6, **4...Kb6 5.Bd8+ Kc6**.

The position in the next diagram is almost the same as our starting position, but the black bishop is at g3, not h2. This small difference allows White to pick up a crucial tempo.

#16a

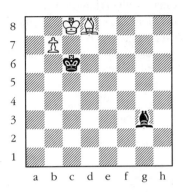

6.Bh4! Bh2 7.Bf2, when the bishop is on his way to a7. Black is one move too late to stop it: **7...Kb5 8.Ba7 Ka6 9.Bb8**.

#16b

Now the black bishop must give way and relocate to a7, which turns out to be a terrible defensive square: **9...Bg1 10.Bg3 Ba7 11.Bf2**, and wins. If 11...Bxf2 12.b8=Q. And if **11...Kb5** we get twelve consecutive moves by the white bishop, **12.Bxa7**.

The next diagram, a 1923 endgame study by Kosek, shows a seven-move knight sequence. Obviously the white pawn cannot be allowed to traverse b7. If that happens, he then makes a new

15

queen. That's why Black must control this square with his king and his bishop. But the blockade at b7 is very tenuous. Once the knight enters the fray, the king will be pushed away from c6, and the bishop will be hanging.

#17
White to Move

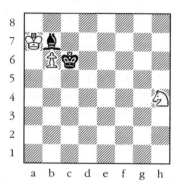

a b c d e f g h

1.Nf5 threatens 2.Ne7+. If 1...Bc8 then 2.Ne7+ (anyway) 2...Kd7 3.Nxc8 Kxc8 4.b7+ and it's all over. This is what Black is trying to avoid, although in the end he finds he cannot. **1...Ba8** A clever attempt. The bishop is immune so long as Black can take the pawn. **2.Nd4+ Kc5 3.Ne6+ Kc6**. Despite the knight checks, Black's king has kept contact with the b6-pawn.

#17a

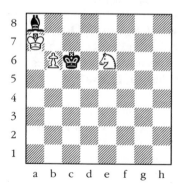

a b c d e f g h

Now White goes after the bishop, forcing it to the more vulnerable square b7: **4.Nc7 Bb7**, and then comes the icing on the cake, **5.Nd5!:**

#17b

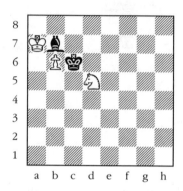

a b c d e f g h

If Black takes the knight, he loses his bishop. If he returns, 5...Ba8, White takes, 6.Kxa8, as his knight now guards his b6-pawn. What's left? Just **5...Bc8 6.Ne7+ Kd7 7.Nxc8 Kxc8** and as we already know **8.b7+** wins easily.

Our final example is a sustained attack by two White knights, featured in the game Capablanca vs. Yates, New York 1924.

#18
White to Move

a b c d e f g h

16

Black just captured a White rook at c4, so White's next is forced, **1.Nxc4**. Here Yates played **1...Bd7** and that allowed Capablanca to go after the weak a5-pawn by **2.Nc3 Rc5** (if 2...Nxc3 3.Rxd7+) **3.Ne4 Rb5 4.Nd6 Rc5 5.Nb7 Rc7 6.Nbxa5.**

Even after the fall of the a-pawn, the knight moves continued, **6...Bb5 7.Nd6 Bd7 8.Nac4 Ra7 9.Ne4**, reaching a total of nine.

As the next diagram shows, Capablanca was a clear pawn ahead with the overall better position. Yates resisted for another thirty moves, then threw in the towel.

Armed as you now are with all this

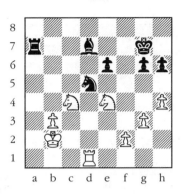

semi-useless information, consider yourself sufficiently warmed up to tackle the main body of mazes in Chapter One. So go on and tackle them; they don't tackle back.

Bishop Mazes

#1

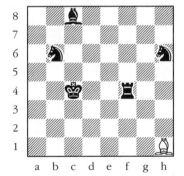

#2

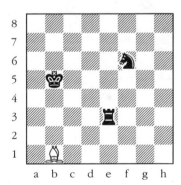

#3

#6

#4

#7

#5

#8

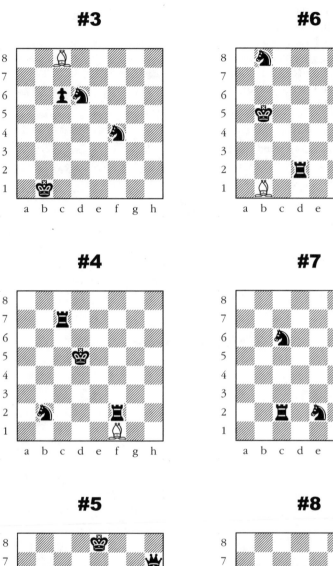

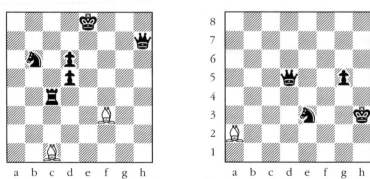

#9

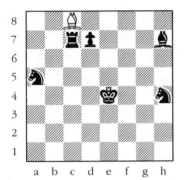

#12

#10

#13

#11

#14

#15

#18

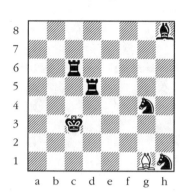

#16

#19

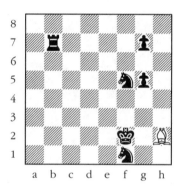

#17

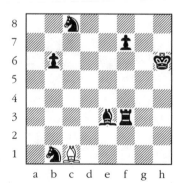

#20

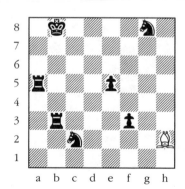

20

#21

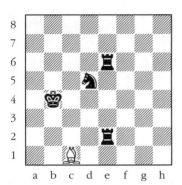

#22

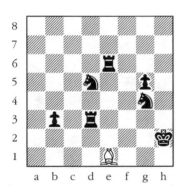

#23

#24

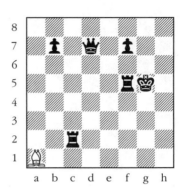

#25

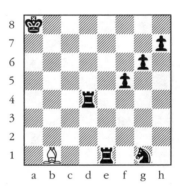

#26

#27

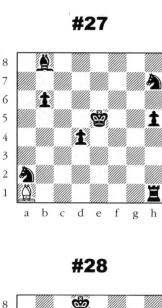

#30

#28

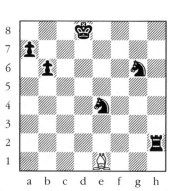

#31

#29

#32

#33

#34

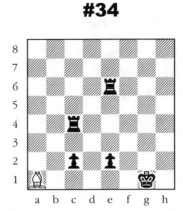

Rook Mazes

#35

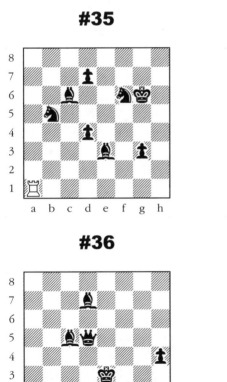

#37

#36

#38

23

#39

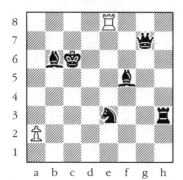

#42

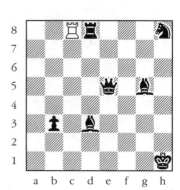

#40

#43

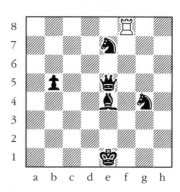

#41

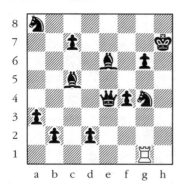

#44

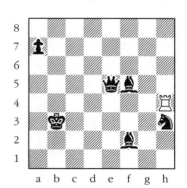

#45

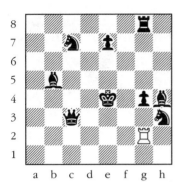

#48

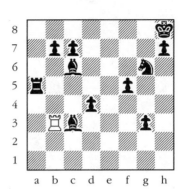

#46

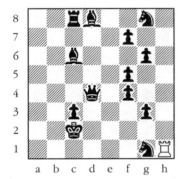

#49

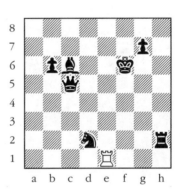

#47

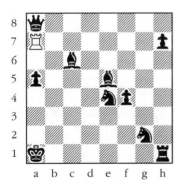

#50

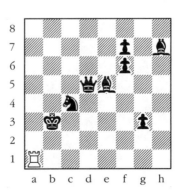

#51

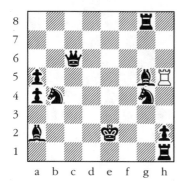

#54

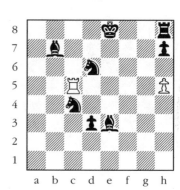

#52

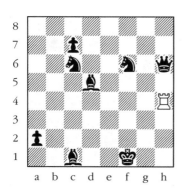

#55

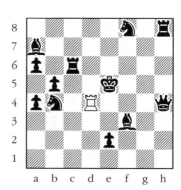

#53

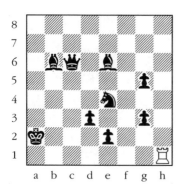

#56

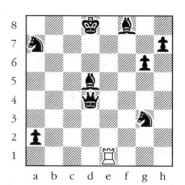

#57

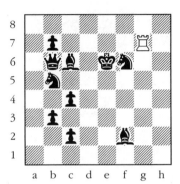

#60

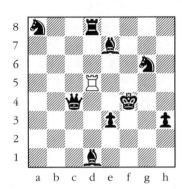

#58

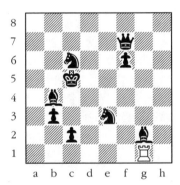

#61

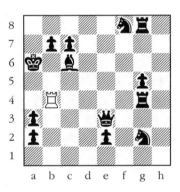

#59

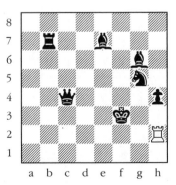

#62

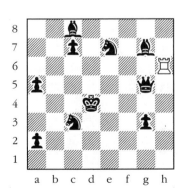

#63

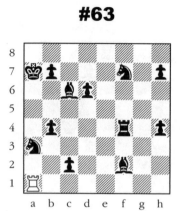

#66

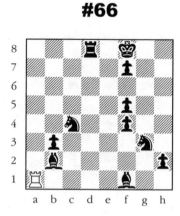

#64

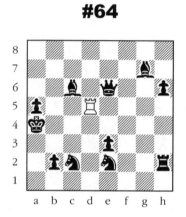

#67

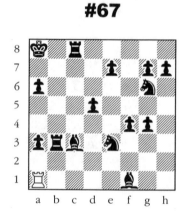

#65

#68

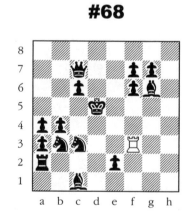

Knight Mazes

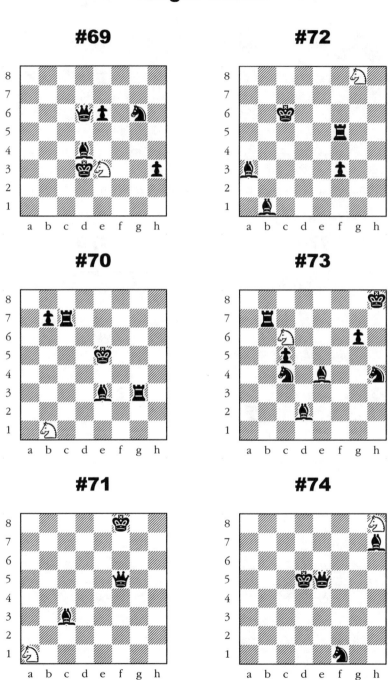

#69

#72

#70

#73

#71

#74

29

#75

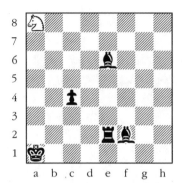

#78

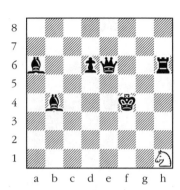

#76

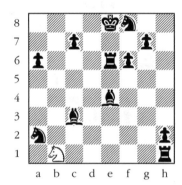

#79

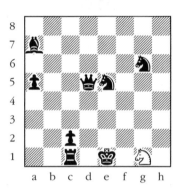

#77

#80

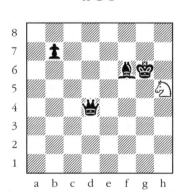

#81

#82

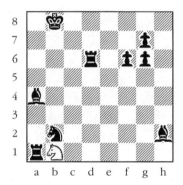

#83

#84

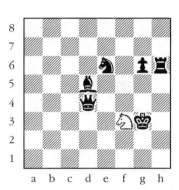

#85

#86

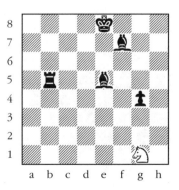

#87

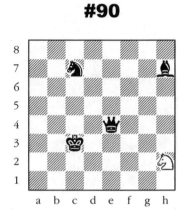

#90

#88

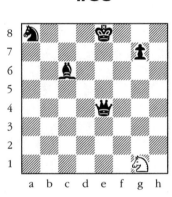

#91

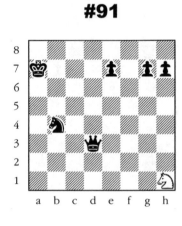

#89

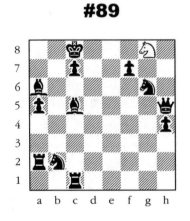

#92

#93

#96

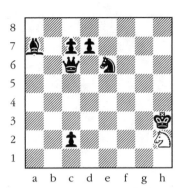

#94

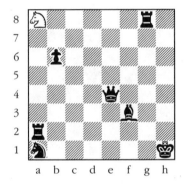

#97

#95

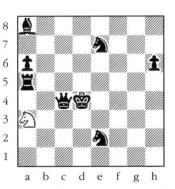

#98

#99

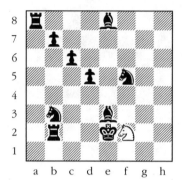

#101

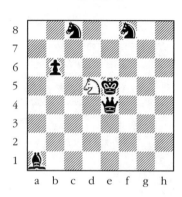

#100

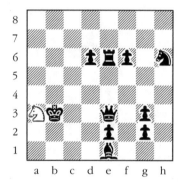

#102

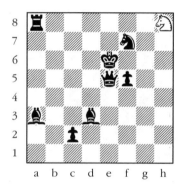

Chapter Two
Queen, Pawn, and King Mazes

The three pieces of Chapter Two fall into a different category than those of Chapter One, and a slight modification of the rules is necessary to accommodate them. The queen, for example, is enormously powerful and for her merely to give check is a waste of her potential. Therefore, we insist that the queen give only checkmate. In fact, check is not allowed.

To assist in giving checkmate, we've provided her (in most cases) with helpers (other White pieces), who can support the queen, take away escape squares, or otherwise pin enemy pieces. The queen's helpers are not allowed to move, give check or checkmate, nor can they be captured.

The king, as you are aware, is unable to march right up to the opposing monarch and attack him directly. It's against the rules as he would be putting himself in check from the enemy king.

A king can only give a discovered check by moving off a line, unmasking a piece in the rear to give the check. Obviously the checking unit has to be a line piece: bishop, rook, or queen.

But that means adding helpers, and once we add helping units, we must go all out for checkmate. A simple straightforward check is forbidden. And as already mentioned, the helping pieces are not permitted to move; nor can they be taken. They are just stationary objects performing their tasks from their starting squares in the diagram. The king's helpers, unlike the queen's, are allowed to give checkmate. In fact it's a requirement; it's the only way checkmate can happen in a king maze.

The pawn is its own special case. One pawn in the field is not much of an attacking force. It sorely needs assistance. Rather than provide aid in the form of other pieces, we decided to simply add more pawns. That way you are allowed to move any or all of your pawns. And you can promote. With that much power on the board even the lowly pawn can give checkmate. So check is out, and checkmate is in.

A special *Chess Mazes* rule about promoted pawns: **Once a pawn is promoted (normally to a queen or knight) it may not move off its promotion square**. It can give checkmate from this square (never check), it can act as a helper, preventing the enemy king's escape, or it can pin down opposing forces. And if you mistakenly promote a pawn on a square where it is *en prise*, then yes, it can be captured. Placing a pawn *en prise* is bad news, regardless of whether it's still a pawn or if it becomes a piece.

Let's review the rules once again, recalling that the major adjustment will be Rule Three.

Rule Number One: White gets queen, king, or pawns to work with, depending on the type of maze. Only White gets to move and he can move only his maze piece. In the case of pawn mazes he can move any and all of his pawns. Helping pieces may never move.

Rule Number Two: Black never moves. The one exception is Rule Number Four.

Rule Number Three: Checking the king is not allowed. The maze is solved when White gives checkmate to the black king. There are no gimmicks here with respect to checkmate. The final position must be a legal checkmate position, such as would occur in an actual game.

Rule Number Four: White is not allowed to place his maze piece (or pawns) on squares where they can be captured. If he does that, places his man *en prise*, Black is allowed to capture and remove the white unit from the board. That's when White loses.

If there are White helpers on the board, pieces or pawns other than the maze piece, Black may not capture them, even if they should happen to be *en prise* in the initial diagram position.

On the other hand if a White maze piece is *en prise* in the initial position, White better use his first move to remove his piece from capture. If he doesn't, Black can take it.

Rule Number Five: Only the shortest solution counts.

That's pretty much the story, so let's look at some **Chess Mazes in Action:**

#19

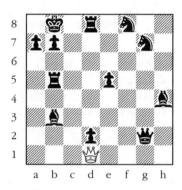

A queen maze. To deliver mate White must capture the d8-rook which means that he must first take the defending h4-bishop. The task then is for the queen to work her way into position so the bishop can be captured. The route is **1.Qa1 2.Qc3 3.Qe3 4.Qh6 5.Qxh4 6.Qxd8#.**

#20

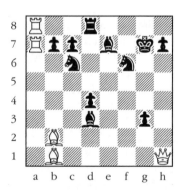

Here it's largely a matter of clearing away the black obstacles so that White's rooks and bishops can exert their power, supporting, pinning, and taking away escape squares.

The solution runs **1.Qd1 2.Qb3 3.Qxb7 4.Qxc6 5.Qxc7 6.Qxd8 7.Qxd4 8.Qxd3 9.Qxh7#.** And yes, it helps to envision the final position before you make move one.

When we come to pawn mazes we observe one significant difference between the pawn and the other pieces. The solutions for bishop, rook, knight, queen, and king mazes are carved in stone, both the moves themselves and the order in which the moves are played. This does not quite hold for pawn mazes. True, the moves given for pawn mazes are the ones that have to be played, but the sequence can be varied. You have some leeway here.

Very often when pawns are marching down the board to make queens, it makes no difference in which order the pawns are advanced. However, we caution you not to be too casual about move order. Some pawn moves simply have to played before others, else pawns would be *en prise* and unable to advance.

This is less confusing than it sounds. Our next example (#21) will make things clear.

1.d3 2.dxe4 3.hxg4. Anything else would put one of White's pawns *en prise*.

#21a

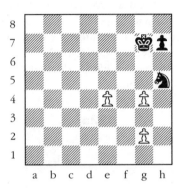

But now White has choices in his move order. If he wants to, he could advance his e-pawn up the board and make a queen. He can also play **3.g5** followed by **4.g4,** and **5.gxh5.**

We'll take the knight directly, **4.gxh5,** then advance the g-pawn, **5.g4 6.g5,** and finally the e-pawn, **7.e5 8.e6 9.e7 10.e8=Q,** finishing up with **11.h6#.**

#22

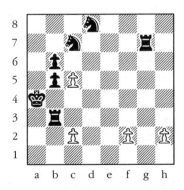

The first move is forced, **1.cxb6,** else White is unable to save his c5-

#21

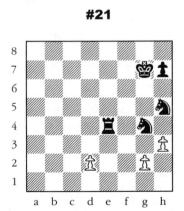

The first three moves are forced,

pawn. The next step is to remove the g7-rook, and since the pawn at f2 is destined to promote at f8, the capture has to be done with the h-pawn.

If White wants to, he could advance the f-pawn up to f6, but he dare not take the rook. We'll go directly with the h-pawn, **2.h4 3.h5 4.h6 5.hxg7**, and now we'll promote, **6.g8=Q**, although there are other options.

#22a

The f-pawn can still advance up to f6, but it can't get past the d8-knight. So we get rid of the knights, **7.bxc7 8.cxd8=Q**. Now the f-pawn goes all the way, **9.f4 10.f5 11.f6 12.f7 13.f8=Q**, and White delivers mate by **14.cxb3#**.

The next diagram is a king maze in which discovered checkmate will be given by the bishop. First the diagonal must be cleared and then the d1-rook eliminated. The solution is **1.Kd3 2.Kxe3 3.Ke4 4.Kxf5 5.Ke4 6.Kd3 7.Kc2 8. Kxd1#**

Note that after taking the f5-rook, the king must retrace his steps exactly. If he leaves the b1-h7 diagonal prematurely, say 5.Kf3, he'd be giving dis-

covered check, and checks of any kind are not admissible.

King Maze
#23

In the next diagram, to release the white pieces, simply round up the black pawns on the e-file and you've got it.

King Maze
#24

1.Kd2 2.Kc3 3.Kc4 4.Kc5 5.Kd6 6.Kxe6 7.Kxe5 8.Kxe4 9.Ke3#.

As noted in the previous chapter, the board generally has to clear out before one piece can suddenly take over and dominate the proceedings.

Here in a pawnless endgame, from

the next diagram, we can see why the queen beats the rook. The black king and rook are separated which suggest that the queen may be able to pick off the rook by a series of checks culminating in a fork.

the white queen has made only one move, Qd1-c2. But starting here she takes over. Of the remaining eleven moves in the game, the queen makes nine, concluding with a burst of five consecutive checks, the last being mate.

#25
White to Move

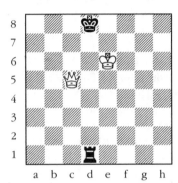

To do this the black king has to be brought to the b-file, when the fork follows at b3. Here's how it's done. **1.Qa5+ Kc8** (If 1…Ke8 2.Qa4+) **2.Qc3+ Kd8 3.Qh8+** (Also strong is 3.Qb3, but White can dispense with subtlety when brute-force checking does the job.) **3…Kc7 4.Qh2+ Kb7** (4…Kd8 is out because of 5.Qb8#, so the king is forced to the b-file). **5.Qb2+ Ka7 6.Qa2+ Kb7 7.Qb3+** and **8.Qxd1**.

But also in the middle game the queen may get opportunities to strut her stuff. It usually happens when she's pursuing an exposed enemy king to his doom. The dexterity of the queen, in being able to switch rapidly from one side of the board to the other, is the telling factor.

Position 26 is from Marshall vs. Gladstone, New York 1932. Up to now

#26
White to Move

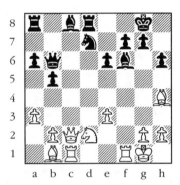

First the black king has to be driven from the h8 corner to the center. That's accomplished by **1.Qh7+ Kf8 2.Qh8+ Ke7 3.Qxg7!** when a break-in at f6 or f7 is inevitable. After **3…Qxe3+ 4.Kh1**, Black decided to allow the entry at f7, **4…Bxh4 5.Qxf7+** and that put his king in the center, subject to further attacks: **5…Kd6 6.Ne4+ Kd5**.

#26a
White to Move

39

The elegant finish was: **7.Qh5+ Bg5 8.Qd1+ Qd4 9.Qb3+ Ke5 10.Qg3+ Kd5 11.Qd6#**.

#26b
Final Position

Sustained play by the pawns can arise either in the opening of the game, or in the endgame. We'll begin with an endgame first examined by the Russian composer Grigoriev in 1930.

#27
White to Move and Win

If White starts with 1.h4, Black's king is too far away to catch it, so he'll have to counter with 1...d5. Then both players will make a queen, White first, but Black with check. The result will be only a draw.

If he starts with his f-pawn, 1.f4, he threatens to queen with check at f8. That will force the black king to come back, 1...Kb4, in order to catch up with the pawn.

This establishes the basic formula. When White moves his h-pawn, Black advances his d-pawn, and when White moves his f-pawn, Black comes back with his king. Astutely jockeying both pawns enables White to win.

1.f4 Kb4 2.h4 d5 3.f5 Kc5 4.h5 d4 5.f6 Kd6 6.h6 d3 7.f7 Ke7 8.h7 d2 9.f8=Q+ This is what it's all about, sacrificing the f-pawn so that the h-pawn can queen with check: **9...Kxf8 10.h8=Q+ Ke7 11.Qd4**. White gathers up the d-pawn and wins easily.

At the start of the game the players generally move some pawns before the pieces come out. How many pawns moves in row can one side make at the start of the game? Apart from nonsense pawn moves, the one recognized opening that comes to mind is the Four Pawns Attack of the Alekhine Defense: **1.e4 Nf6 2.e5 Nd5 3.d4 d6 4.c4 Nb6 5.f4 dxe5 6.fxe5**.

#28
Black to Move

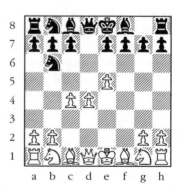

40

That's six pawn moves in a row, and if Black continues **6...c5** from diagram #28, White can add another with **7.d5**. That would appear to be the limit, at least for sound, sensible openings.

Should the opponent prove cooperative, then it is possible to squeeze out even more pawn moves. Marshall (again) shows how to do it, vs. Rogosin, New York 1940. The opening was the Sicilian Wing Gambit **1.e4 c5 2.b4!? cxb4 3.a3** which, while not 100% correct, poses plenty of problems at the board.

His opponent quickly became confused and mishandled his knights: **3...Nc6 4.axb4 Nf6 5.b5 Nd4 6.c3 Ne6 7.e5 Nd5 8.c4 Ndf4 9.g3 Ng6 10.f4**.

#29
after 10.f4

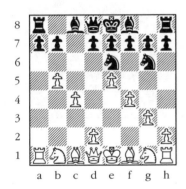

The threat is 11.f5. Since 10...Nc7 11.f5 Nxe5 12.d4 still drops a knight, Black decided to get two pawns for his piece, **10...Ngxf4 11.gxf4 Nxf4 12.d4 Ng6 13.h4 e6 14.h5 Bb4+** (see next diagram).

White is about to play 15.hxg6, but Black's check (14...Bb4+) breaks the

string of pawn moves at fourteen. Since we're over halfway there we'll give the rest of the game for the sake of completeness.

#29a
after 14...Bb4+

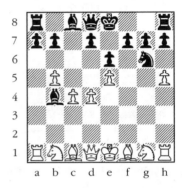

15.Bd2 Bxd2+ 16.Nxd2 Ne7 17.Ne4 Nf5 18.h6! intending to answer 18...Nxh6 with 19.Nd6+ Ke7 20.Rxh6 gxh6 21.Qh5 and a vicious attack.

#29c
after 18.h6

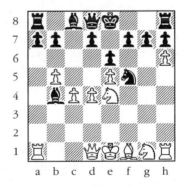

Black's reply, **18...g6**, opened up a new square for White's knight and the exchange of queens that follows shortly thereafter in no way reduces White's pressure. **19.Nf6+ Kf8 20.Nf3 d6 21.Ng5 dxe5 22.dxe5 Qxd1+ 23.Rxd1**

41

Ke7 24.Rh3 b6 25.Bg2 Rb8 26.Ngxh7
and Black resigns.

#29d
Final Position

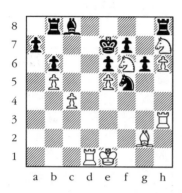

He can't move his bishop: 26...Bb7
27.Rd7#. And if he challenges for the
d-file, 26...Rd8, there follows 27.Rxd8
Kxd8 28.Nf8 with advance of the h-
pawn.

The ending is the domain of the
king. As the pieces get knocked off the
board and the likelihood of checkmate
recedes into the background, it's generally safe for the king to poke his head
out and participate in the struggle. Of
course, even then the king is not immune to attack, but checks are mere
pinpricks when there is no checkmate
to follow. Let's see how the king deals
with checks.

In the next diagram, Black's initial
move, **1...e2**, places his pawn one
square away from queening. We've already seen how a queen can beat a rook.

Can White stop the pawn? Not in
any obvious way since his rook is badly
placed. He can't bring the rook in front
of the pawn, nor behind it.

#30
Black to Move

About all he can do is give check,
2.Rb3+ and see where Black puts his
king.

#30a
after 2.Rb3+

This check has to be answered very
carefully. Black can lose if he elects
2...Kc4? allowing 3.Re3. Somewhat
better, but only drawing is 2...Ke4. That
permits the rook to get behind the pawn
by 3. Rb8 Kf3 (definitely not 3...e1=Q?
4.Re8+ K-any and 5.Rxe1) 4.Re8 and
the rook can always give itself up for
the pawn, Rxe2, if he has to. Equally
unconvincing is 2...Kd2, for pretty
much the same reason, 3.Rb8 e1=Q
4.Rd8+ Ke2 5.Re8+ and 6.Rxe1.

42

That leaves **2...Kd4! 3.Rb4+ Kd5 4.Rb5+ Kd6 5.Rb6+ Ke7.**

#30b
after 5...Ke7

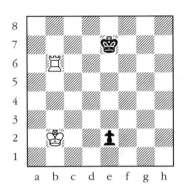

Now it's safe to play on to the e-file. With the king at e7, the rook is unable to get to e8. Still, White can continue checking: **6.Rb7+ Kf6 7.Rb6+ Kf5 8.Rb5+ Kf4 9.Rb4+ Kf3 10.Rb3+ Kf2**, when the checks run out. We don't count the frivolous 11.Rf3+ Kxf3.

It turns out that not only the rook, but also the white king is on a poor square. Had the king been on a2, White could still make a draw by pinning the pawn, 11.Rb2. Alas, the king has already reserved b2 for himself.

We close the chapter with a rare offensive king march in the middle game.

The next diagram is from Short vs. Timman, Tilburg 1991, where White undoubtedly has the advantage. He has full control of the d-file, preventing the black rooks from becoming active, and he has a dark square bind on the kingside, Black having placed his pawns on light colored squares.

#31
White to Move

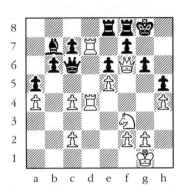

But how to realize the advantage? The otherwise attractive move 1.Ng5, threatening f7, is unplayable because of 1...Qxg2#.

Surely we have given you the clue to figure it out. Short did it at the board, **1.Kh2!! Rc8** (If 1...Bc8 2.Ng5! Bxd7 3.Rf4! and wins.) **2.Kg3 Rce8 3.Kf4 Bc8 4.Kg5** and Timman resigned.

#31a
after 4.Kg5

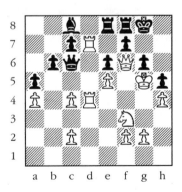

The only way to stop 5.Kh6 and 6.Qg7# is by 4...Kh7. But there are a couple of problems with that move. First there's 5.Rxf7+ Rxf7 6.Qxf7+ Kh8 7.Kh6, with mate in just a few

43

more moves. Second, White may also play 5.Qxg6+ Kh8 6.Qh6+ Kg8 7.Kf6 and again Qg7 mate is coming.

Having accumulated still more information (this time we won't categorize it) you are certainly ready to start solving the mazes of Chapter Two.

A cautionary note. The mazes here tend to run longer than those in the previous chapter, and require more visualization skills to grasp the final mating position. But if you've come this far, you should be up to the task. So, go ahead, solve some mazes.

Queen Mazes

#103

#105

#104

#106

44

#107

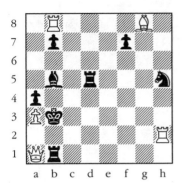

#110

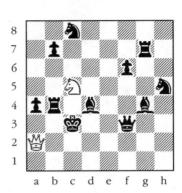

#108

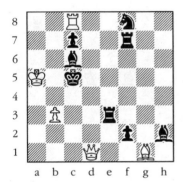

#111

#109

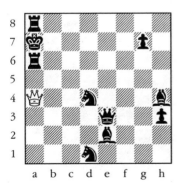

#112

#113

#114

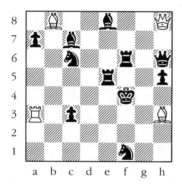

#115

#116

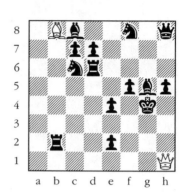

#117

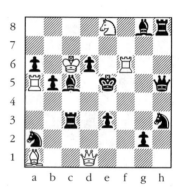

#118

46

#119

#120

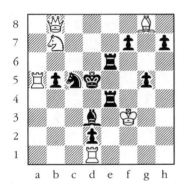

#121

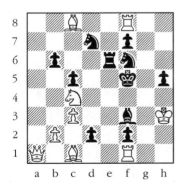

#122

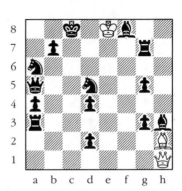

#123

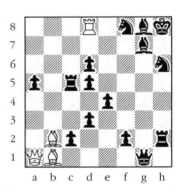

#124

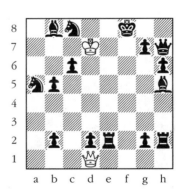

#125

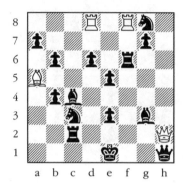

#128

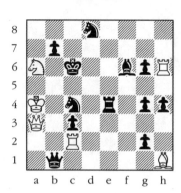

#126

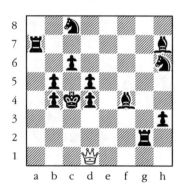

#129

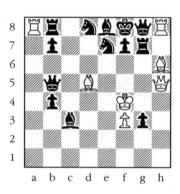

#127

#130

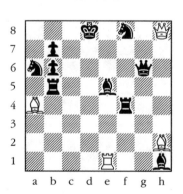

48

#131

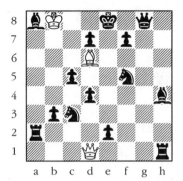

#134

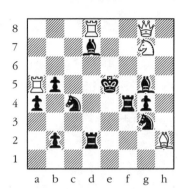

#132

#135

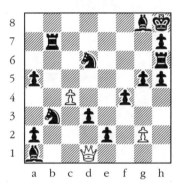

#133

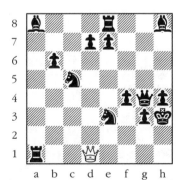

#136

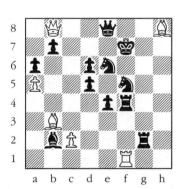

Pawn Mazes

#137

#140

#138

#141

#139

#142

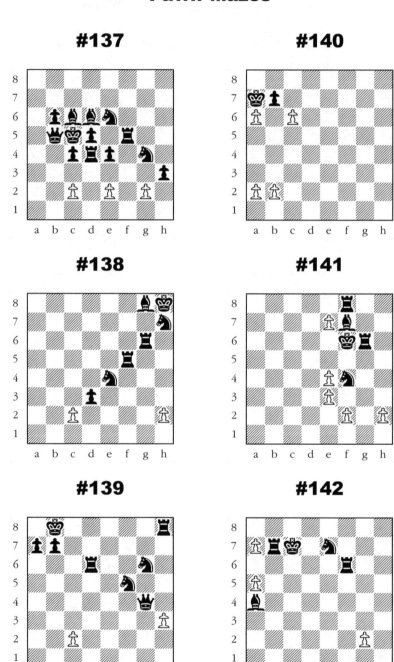

#143

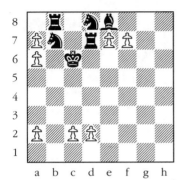

#146

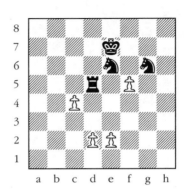

#144

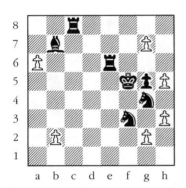

#147

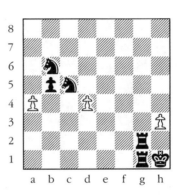

#145

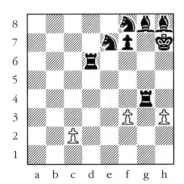

#148

#149

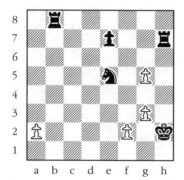

#152

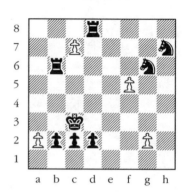

#150

#153

#151

#154

#155

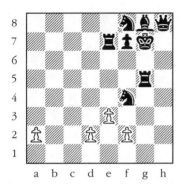

#158

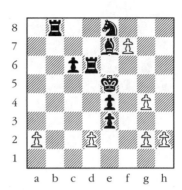

#156

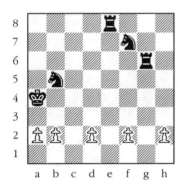

#159

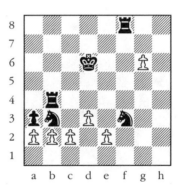

#157

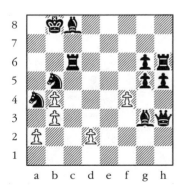

#160

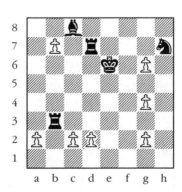

#161

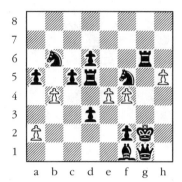

#164

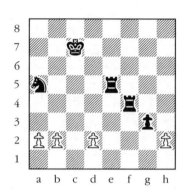

#162

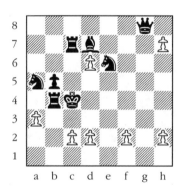

#165

#163

#166

#167

#169

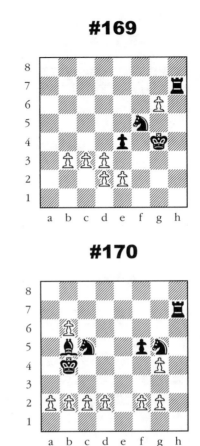

#168

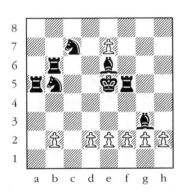

#170

King Mazes

#171

#172

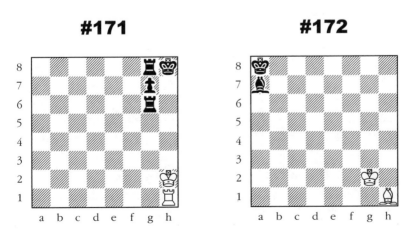

55

#173

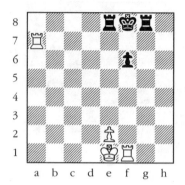

#176

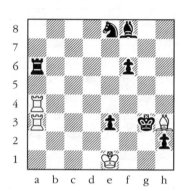

#174

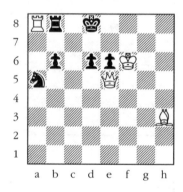

#177

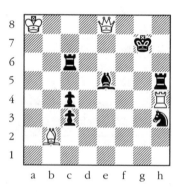

#175

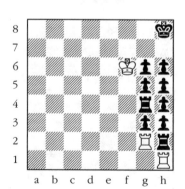

#178

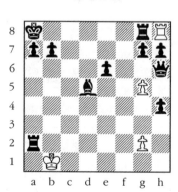

#179

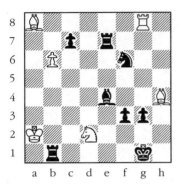

#182

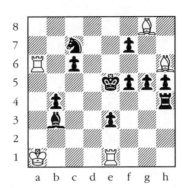

#180

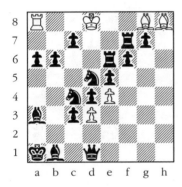

#183

#181

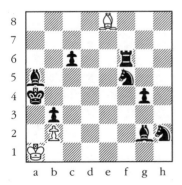

#184

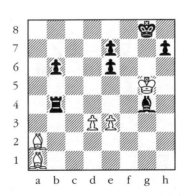

#185

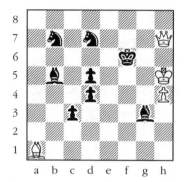

#188

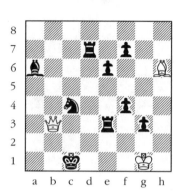

#186

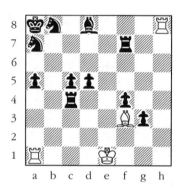

#189

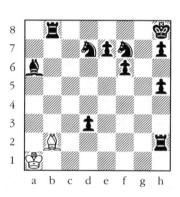

#187

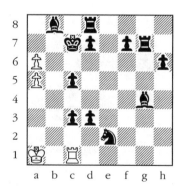

#190

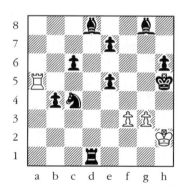

#191

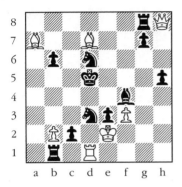

#194

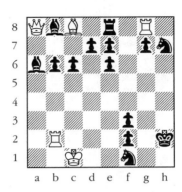

#192

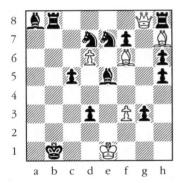

#195

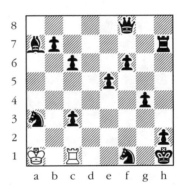

#193

#196

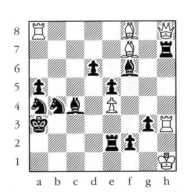

#197

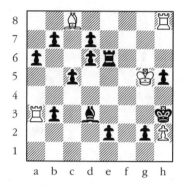

#198

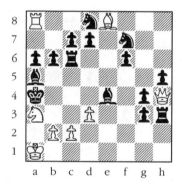

#199

#200

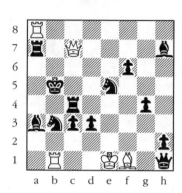

#201

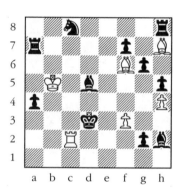

#202

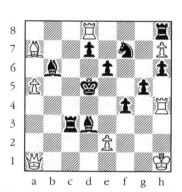

#203

#204

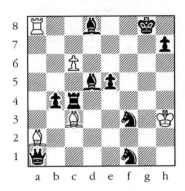

61

Solutions: Bishop Mazes

#1

1.Bc6 2.Be8 3.Bh5 4.Be2+

#2

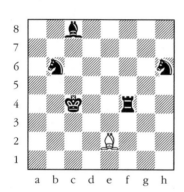

1.Bf5 2.Bc8 3.Bb7 4.Bg2 5.Bf1+

#3

1.Bg4 2.Bd1 3.Bb3 4.Bg8 5.Bh7+

#4

1.Bb5 2.Be8 3.Bg6 4.Bb1 5.Ba2+

#5

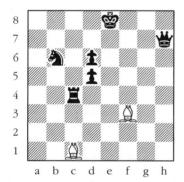

You need to work with both bishops. The dark-squared bishop knocks out the guard on b6; the light-squared guy cleans up and gives the fatal check.
1.Be3 2.Bxb6 3.Bxd5 4.Bxc4 5.Bb5+

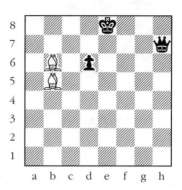

#6

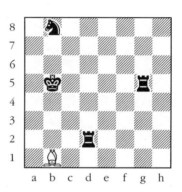

1.Be4 2.Bb7 3.Bc8 4.Bh3 5.Bf1+

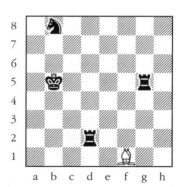

63

#7

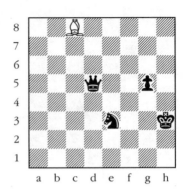

1.Bg7 2.Bf8 3.Bd6 4.Bc7 5.Bb6 6.Be3+

#9

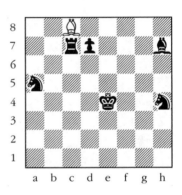

1.Ba6 2.Be2 3.Bh5 4.Bf7 5.Ba2 6.Bb1+

#8

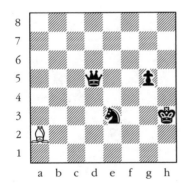

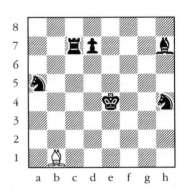

1.Bb1 2.Bg6 3.Bh5 4.Be2 5.Ba6 6.Bc8+

#10

1.Bf5 2.Bh3 3.Bf1 4.Bb5 5.Be8
6.Bf7+

#11

1.Bg8 2.Bh7 3.Bd3 4.Ba6 5.Bc8
6.Bh3 7.Bg2+

#12

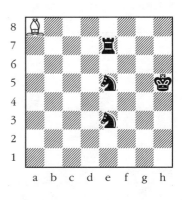

1.Be4 2.Bb1 3.Ba2 4.Bb3 5.Ba4
6.Bb5 7.Be2+

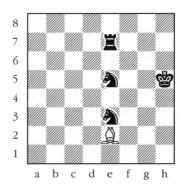

#13

1.Bd5 2.Bg8 3.Bh7 4.Bc2 5.Ba4 6.Be8 7.Bh5+

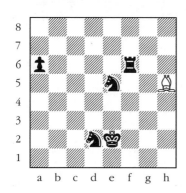

#14

1.Bg5 2.Bh4 3.Be1 4.Bc3 5.Bd4 6.Bg1 7.Bh2+

#15

1.Bg8 2.Bh7 3.Bc2 4.Bd1 5.Bg4 6.Bh3 7.Bg2+

#16

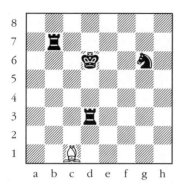

**1.Bg5 2.Bd8 3.Ba5 4.Be1 5.Bf2
6.Bg1 7.Bh2+**

#18

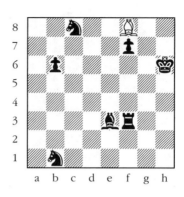

#17

**1.Ba7 2.Bb8 3.Bf4 4.Bc1 5.Ba3
6.Be7 7.Bh4 8.Be1+**

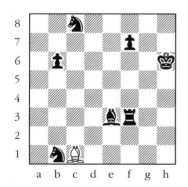

**1.Bb2 2.Be5 3.Bc7 4.Bd8 5.Bh4
6.Be1 7.Bb4 8.Bf8+**

#19

1.Be5 2.Bc3 3.Ba5 4.Bd8 5.Bxg5 6.Bc1 7.Ba3 8.Bc5+

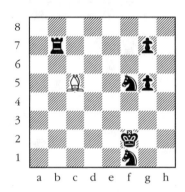

#20

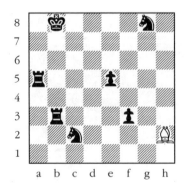

1.Bg3 2.Bh4 3.Bd8 4.Bxa5 5.Bd8 6.Bh4 7.Bg3 8.Bxe5+

#21

1.Bg5 2.Bh4 3.Bg3 4.Bb8 5.Ba7 6.Bd4 7.Bg7 8.Bf8+

#22

1.Ba5 2.Bd8 3.Bxg5 4.Bc1 5.Ba3
6.Bc5 7.Ba7 8.Bb8+

#24

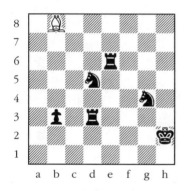

1.Bg7 2.Bf8 3.Bb4 4.Be1 5.Bg3
6.Bb8 7.Ba7 8.Be3+

#23

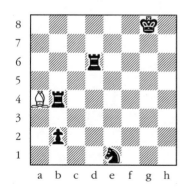

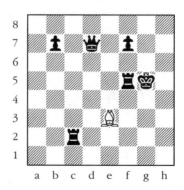

1.Be8 2.Bh5 3.Be2 4.Bf1 5.Bh3
6.Bf5 7.Bb1 8.Ba2+

#25

1.Ba2 2.Bg8 3.Bxh7 4.Bxg6 5.Bxf5
6.Bc8 7.Ba6 8.Bb5 9.Bc6+

#27

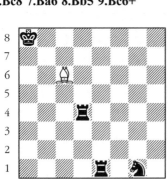

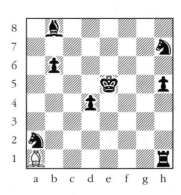

1.Bb2 2.Ba3 3.Be7 4.Bd8 5.Bxb6
6.Ba5 7.Bd2 8.Bh6 9.Bg7+

#26

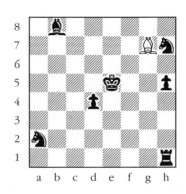

1.Bg6 2.Be8 3.Ba4 4.Bd1 5.Bg4
6.Bc8 7.Ba6 8.Bf1 9.Bg2+

#28

1.Bb4 2.Ba3 3.Bc1 4.Be3 5.Bg1
6.Bxh2 7.Bb8 8.Bxa7 9.Bxb6+

#30

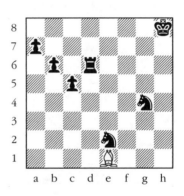

1.Bh4 2.Be7 3.Bxd6 4.Bb8 5.Bxa7
6.Bxb6 7.Bxc5 8.Ba3 9.Bb2+

#29

1.Bh5 2.Bd1 3.Bc2 4.Bf5 5.Bxc8
6.Bf5 7.Bh7 8.Bg8 9.Bd5+

#31

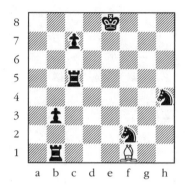

1.Ba6 2.Bc8 3.Be6 4.Bg8 5.Bh7
6.Bxb1 7.Bh7 8.Bg8 9.Bxb3 10.Ba4+

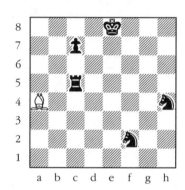

#32

1.Bh6 2.Bf8 3.Bb4 4.Be1 5.Bh4
6.Bd8 7.Bb6 8.Bg1 9.Bh2 10.Bxe5+

#33

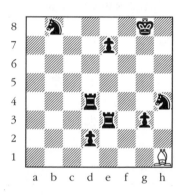

1.Bb7 2.Bc8 3.Bh3 4.Bf1 5.Bb5
6.Be8 7.Bh5 8.Bd1 9.Bc2 10.Bb1
11.Ba2+

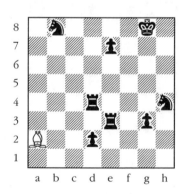

#34

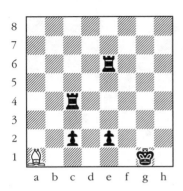

1.Bg7 2.Bf8 3.Ba3 4.Bc1 5.Bg5

6.Bd8 7.Ba5 8.Be1 9.Bg3 10.Bb8 11.Ba7+

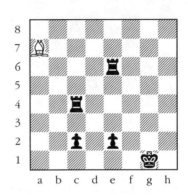

Solutions: Rook Mazes

#35

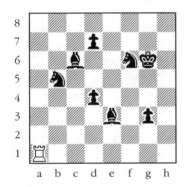

1.Ra6 2.Rb6 3.Rb8 4.Rh8 5.Rh3 6.Rxg3+

#36

1.Rf1 2.Rf6 3.Ra6 4.Ra1 5.Rc1 6.Rc3+

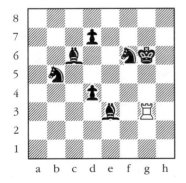

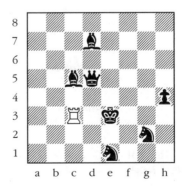

#37

1.Rxa8 2.Rxa1 3.Rg1 4.Rxg5 5.Rxb5 6.Rxb3+

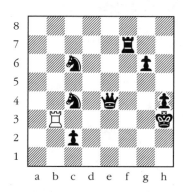

#38

1.Rb5 2.Ra5 3.Ra7 4.Rh7 5.Rh5 6.Rf5 7.Rf8+

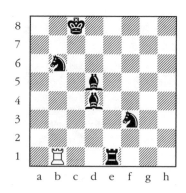

#39

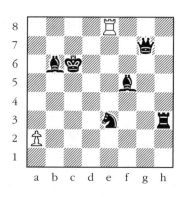

1.Ra8 2.Ra4 3.Rf4 4.Rf2 5.Re2 6.Re1 7.Rc1+

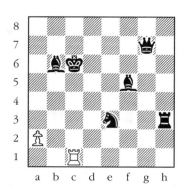

74

#40

1.Rh5 2.Re5 3.Re4 4.Ra4 5.Ra8
6.Rh8 7.Rh7 8.Rxg7+

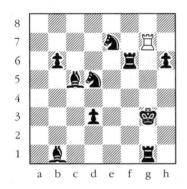

#41

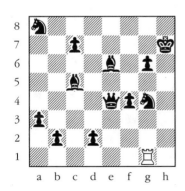

1.Rd1 2.Rxd2 3.Rd8 4.Rb8 5.Rb5
6.Rxc5 7.Rc3 8.Rh3+

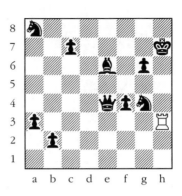

#42

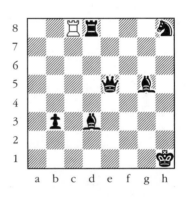

1.Rc6 2.Rb6 3.Rxb3 4.Ra3 5.Ra2
6.Rf2 7.Rf3 8.Rh3+

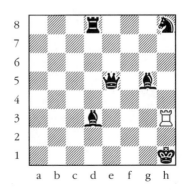

#43

1.Rd8 2.Rd7 3.Ra7 4.Ra3 5.Rh3
6.Rh4 7.Rxg4 8.Rg1+

#44

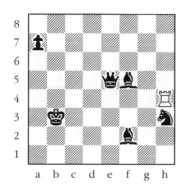

1.Rh6 2.Rc6 3.Rc1 4.Rd1 5.Rd8
6.Rf8 7.Rf7 8.Rb7+

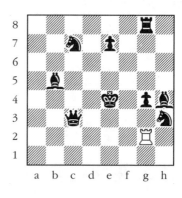

#45

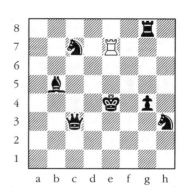

1.Ra2 2.Ra7 3.Rb7 4.Rb6 5.Rh6
6.Rxh4 7.Rh7 8.Rxe7+

#46

1.Rh7 2.Rxf7 3.Rf8 4.Rxg8
5.Rxg6 6.Re6 7.Re1 8.Ra1 9.Ra2+

#47

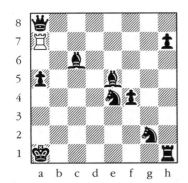

1.Re7 2.Rxe5 3.Re7 4.Rg7 5.Rxg2
6.Rg4 7.Rxf4 8.Rf3 9.Ra3+

#48

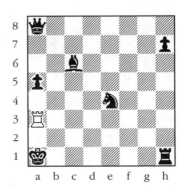

1.Rb1 2.Rc1 3.Rc2 4.Re2 5.Re6
6.Rf6 7.Rf7 8.Rxc7 9.Rc8+

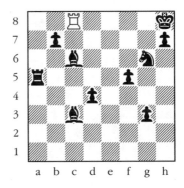

#49

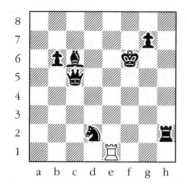

1.Ra1 2.Ra7 3.Rc7 4.Rc8 5.Rd8
6.Rd3 7.Rg3 8.Rg4 9.Rf4+

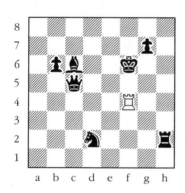

#50

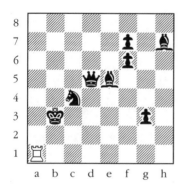

1.Ra7 2.Re7 3.Re8 4.Rh8 5.Rxh7
6.Rh5 7.Rf5 8.Rf1 9.Rb1+

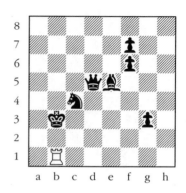

#51

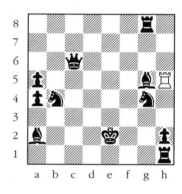

1.Rh3 2.Rg3 3.Rxg4 4.Rg3 5.Rh3
6.Rh7 7.Ra7 8.Rxa5 9.Re5+

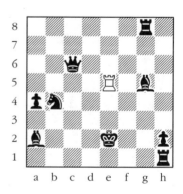

78

#52

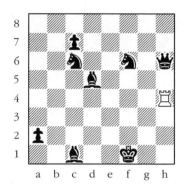

1.Ra4 2.Ra8 3.Rc8 4.Rxc7 5.Rb7
6.Rb5 7.Rc5 8.Rc3 9.Rd3 10.Rd1+

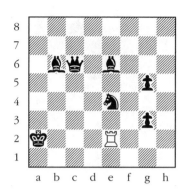

#54

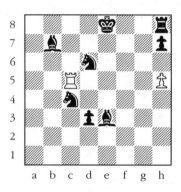

1.Rc7 2.Rg7 3.Rg3 4.Rh3 5.Rh2
6.Ra2 7.Ra1 8.Rf1 9.Rf6 10.Re6+

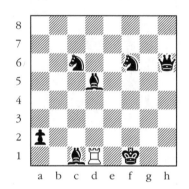

#53

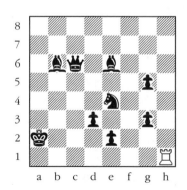

1.Rh8 2.Rf8 3.Rf3 4.Rxd3 5.Rf3
6.Rf8 7.Rh8 8.Rh1 9.Re1 10.Rxe2+

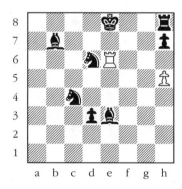

79

#55

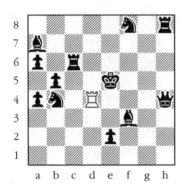

11.Rxf8+

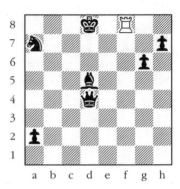

1.Rd2 2.Rb2 3.Rb1 4.Ra1 5.Ra3
6.Rxf3 7.Rf7 8.Rxa7 9.Ra8 10.Re8+

#57

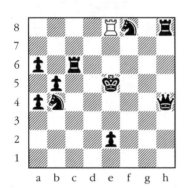

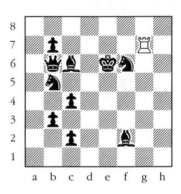

1.Rg6 2.Rh6 3.Rh8 4.Ra8 5.Ra4
6.Rxc4 7.Rb4 8.Rxb3 9.Rb2 10.Rxc2
11.Re2+

#56

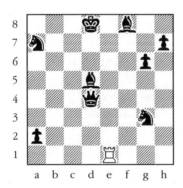

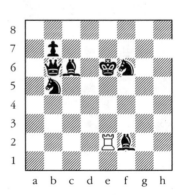

1.Rc1 2.Rc2 3.Rh2 4.Rh3 5.Rxg3
6.Rh3 7.Rh2 8.Rc2 9.Rc1 10.Rf1

80

#58

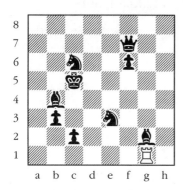

1.Ra1 2.Ra8 3.Rh8 4.Rh4 5.Rf4
6.Rf2 7.Re2 8.Rxe3 9.Re2 10.Rf2
11.Rf5+

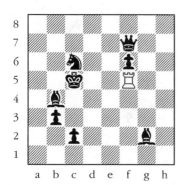

#59

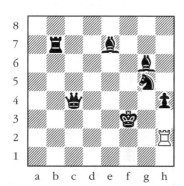

1.Rh1 2.Ra1 3.Ra8 4.Rh8 5.Rh6

6.Rxg6 7.Rh6 8.Rh8 9.Ra8 10.Ra5
11.Rf5+

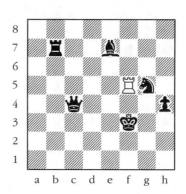

#60

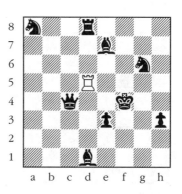

1.Ra5 2.Ra1 3.Rb1 4.Rb2 5.Rh2
6.Rxh3 7.Rh6 8.Rxg6 9.Rg7 10.Rxe7
11.Rh7 12.Rh4+

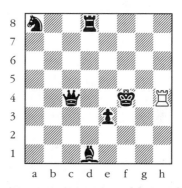

#61

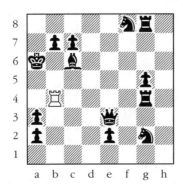

1.Rxg4 2.Rc4 3.Rc2 4.Rxa2 5.Ra1
6.Rh1 7.Rh6 8.Rf6 9.Rf7 10.Rxc7
11.Rc8 12.Ra8+

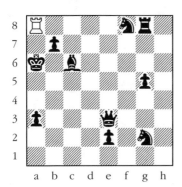

#62

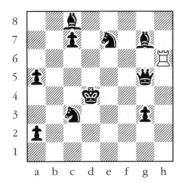

1.Rh1 2.Rg1 3.Rg2 4.Rb2 5.Rb8

6.Ra8 7.Ra7 8.Rxc7 9.Ra7 10.Ra8
11.Rb8 12.Rb6 13.Rd6+

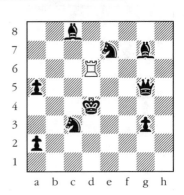

#63

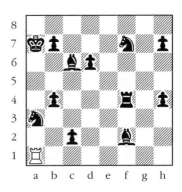

1.Ra2 2.Rb2 3.Rb3 4.Rd3 5.Rd2
6.Re2 7.Re7 8.Rc7 9.Rc8 10.Rg8
11.Rg7 12.Rxh7 13.Rh5 14.Ra5+

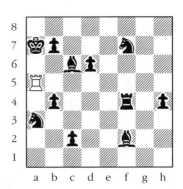

#64

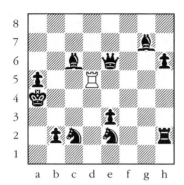

**1.Rd8 2.Rb8 3.Rb6 4.Ra6 5.Ra7
6.Rxg7 7.Rh7 8.Rh8 9.Rb8 10.Rxb2
(Or 7.Ra7 8.Ra6 9.Rb6 10.Rxb2)
11.Rxc2 12.Rb2 13.Rb1 14.Ra1+**

#65

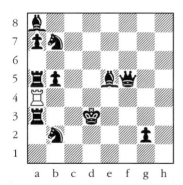

1.Rh4 2.Rh6 3.Rc6 4.Rc1 5.Rg1

**6.Rxg2 7.Rg8 8.Rxa8 9.Re8 10.Re7
11.Rxb7 12.Re7 13.Re8 14.Rd8+**

#66

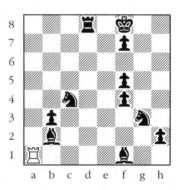

**1.Ra6 2.Rh6 3.Rh4 4.Rxf4 5.Rf3
6.Rxg3 7.Rf3 8.Rxf1 9.Rf4 10.Rxc4
11.Rb4 12.Rxb3 13.Rxb2 14.Rxh2
15.Rh8+**

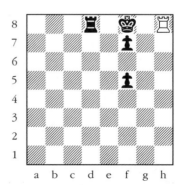

#67

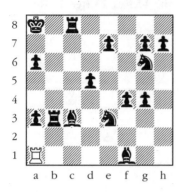

#68

1.Ra2 2.Rh2 3.Rxh7 4.Rh5 5.Rg5
6.Rxg6 7.Re6 8.Rxe7 9.Rf7 10.Rxf4
11.Rf7 12.Re7 13.Rxe3 14.Re7 (Or
14.Rg3 15.Rg1 16.Rxf1) 15.Rf7
16.Rxf1 17.Rf4 18.Ra4 19.Rxa6+

1.Rh3 2.Rh4 3.Rxb4 4.Rh4 5.Rh3
6.Rxc3 7.Rh3 8.Rh8 9.Rg8 10.Rxg7
11.Rg8 12.Ra8 13.Rxa4 14.Rb4
15.Rxb3 16.Rf3 17.Rxf6 18.Rf3
19.Rc3 20.Rxc1 21.Rg1 22.Rg5+.

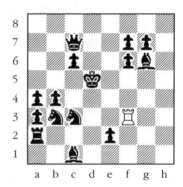

84

Solutions: Knight Mazes

#69

1.Na3 2.Nb5 3.Nxc7 4.Nb5 5.Na3 6.Nc4+

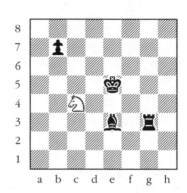

1.Ng4 2.Nh6 3.Nf7 4.Ng5 5.Nf3 6.Ne1+

#71

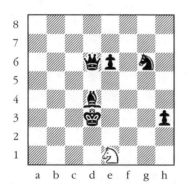

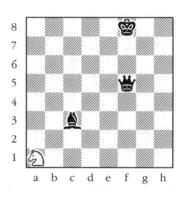

#70

1.Nb3 2.Nc1 3.Ne2 4.Ng3 5.Nxf5 6.Nh4 7.Ng6+

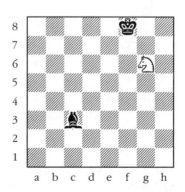

#72

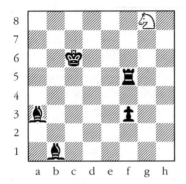

**1.Nh6 2.Ng4 3.Nh2 4.Nf1 5.Nd2
6.Nb3 7.Nd4+**

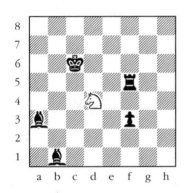

#73

**1.Nd8 2.Ne6 3.Nxc5 4.Nxe4 5.Nc5
6.Nxb7 7.Nd8 8.Nf7+**

#74

**1.Nf7 2.Nd8 3.Nb7 4.Na5 5.Nb3
6.Nc1 7.Na2 8.Nb4+**

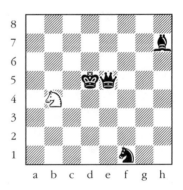

86

#75

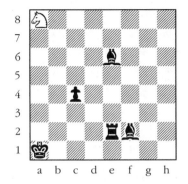

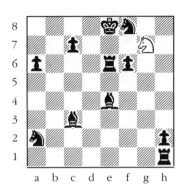

1.Nc7 2.Nb5 3.Nc3 4.Nxe2 5.Nc3
6.Nb5 7.Na3 8.Nc2+

#77

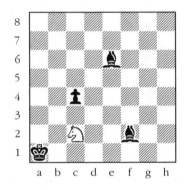

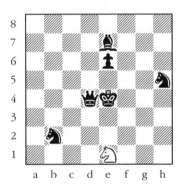

1.Nc2 2.Na1 3.Nb3 4.Na5 5.Nc6
6.Nxe7 7.Ng8 8.Nxh6 9.Nf7 10.Ng5+

#76

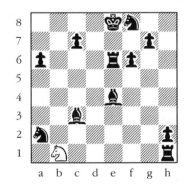

1.Na3 2.Nc4 3.Ne3 4.Ng4 5.Nf2
6.Nh3 7.Nf4 8.Nh5 9.Nxg7+

#78

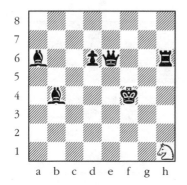

11.Nxc2+

1.Nf2 2.Nd1 3.Nb2 4.Na4 5.Nb6
6.Na8 7.Nc7 8.Nxa6 9.Nxb4 10.Nd3+

#80

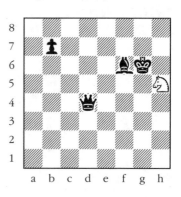

1.Ng3 2.Nf1 3.Nh2 4.Nf3 5.Ne1
6.Nc2 7.Na3 8.Nb5 9.Nc7 10.Ne6
11.Nf8+

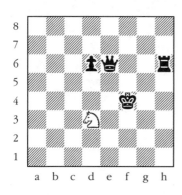

#79

1.Nh3 2.Ng5 3.Nh7 4.Nf6 5.Nxd5
6.Nc3 7.Na2 8.Nxc1 9.Nb3 10.Na1

88

#81

1.Na3 2.Nc4 3.Nb6 4.Nd7 5.Nf8
6.Nxh7 7.Ng5 8.Nf3 9.Nxe1 10.Nd3
11.Nf2+

#82

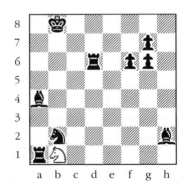

1.Nc3 2.Ne4 3.Nf2 4.Ng4 5.Nxh2
6.Ng4 7.Nf2 8.Ne4 9.Nxd6 10.Ne4

11.Nc5 12.Na6+

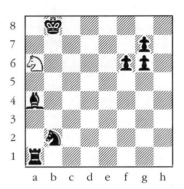

#83

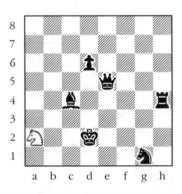

1.Nb4 2.Nc6 3.Nb8 4.Nd7 5.Nf8
6.Ng6 7.Nxh4 8.Ng6 9.Nf8 10.Nd7
11.Nb6 12.Nxc4+

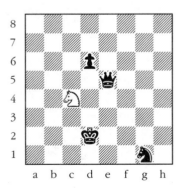

89

#84

1.Ne1 2.Nc2 3.Na3 4.Nb5 5.Nd6
6.Nf7 7.Nxh6 8.Ng8 9.Ne7 10.Nxg6
11.Ne7 12.Nf5+

#86

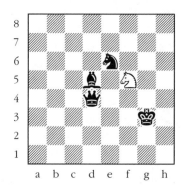

#85

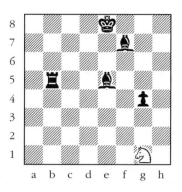

1.Ne2 2.Nc1 3.Nd3 4.Ne1 5.Nc2
6.Na3 7.Nxb5 8.Na7 9.Nc6 10.Nxe5
11.Nxg4 12.Nf6+

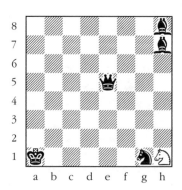

1.Nf2 2.Ng4 3.Nh6 4.Nf7 5.Nd8
6.Nc6 7.Na7 8.Nc8 9.Nb6 10.Nc4

#87

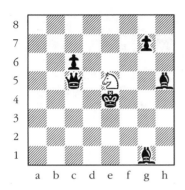

1.Nd7 2.Nb8 3.Na6 4.Nc7 5.Ne6
6.Nxg7 7.Ne6 8.Nc7 9.Na6 10.Nb8
11.Nd7 12.Nf6+

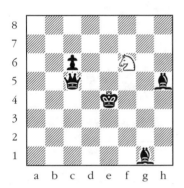

#88

1.Nh3 2.Nf2 3.Nd1 4.Nc3 5.Na2
6.Nc1 7.Nb3 8.Nd2 9.Nf1 10.Ng3

11.Nh5 12.Nxg7+

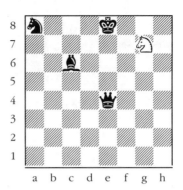

#89

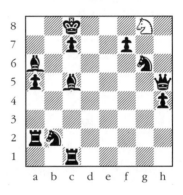

1.Nf6 2.Nxh5 3.Nf6 4.Ne4 5.Nd2
6.Nb3 7.Nxc1 8.Nb3 9.Nxc5 10.Nb3
11.Nd4 12.Nc6 13.Na7+

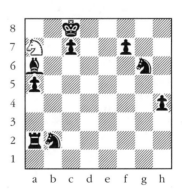

#90

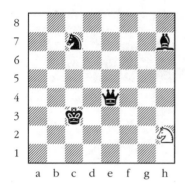

1.Nf1 2.Ng3 3.Nh5 4.Nf6 5.Nd7
6.Nb6 7.Nc8 8.Nd6 9.Nf7 10.Ng5
11.Nh3 12.Nf2 13.Nd1+

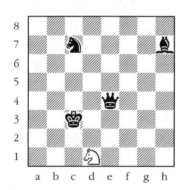

#91

1.Nf2 2.Ng4 3.Ne5 4.Nf7 5.Ng5
6.Ne6 7.Nxg7 8.Ne6 9.Ng5 10.Nf7

11.Nh6 12.Ng8 13.Nxe7 14.Nc8+

#92

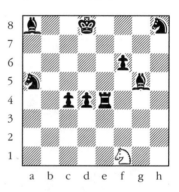

1.Ng3 2.Nh1 3.Nf2 4.Nd1 5.Nb2
6.Na4 7.Nb6 8.Nxa8 9.Nb6 10.Na4
11.Nc5 12.Nxe4 13.Nc5 14.Ne6+

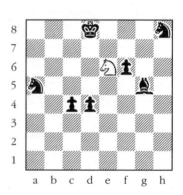

#93

1.Nf7 2.Ne5 3.Nd3 4.Nc1 5.Ne2
6.Nc3 7.Nb5 8.Nxa7 9.Nc8 10.Nxe7
11.Nc8 12.Nd6 13.Ne8 14.Nf6+

#94

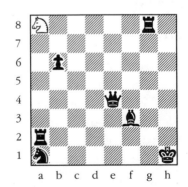

1.Nc7 2.Nb5 3.Nc3 4.Nxa2 5.Nc3
6.Nb5 7.Nd6 8.Nf7 9.Nh6 10.Nxg8

11.Nh6 12.Nf7 13.Ng5 14.Nh3
15.Nf2+

#95

1.Nb1 2.Nd2 3.Nf1 4.Nh2 5.Ng4
6.Nf6 7.Nd7 8.Nb6 9.Nxa8 10.Nb6
11.Nd7 12.Nf6 13.Ng4 14.Nh2
15.Nf3+

#96

1.Nf1 2.Nd2 3.Nb3 4.Nc1 5.Nd3 6.Ne5 7.Ng6 8.Ne7 9.Nc8 10.Nxa7 11.Nc8 12.Ne7 13.Ng6 14.Ne5 15.Nd3 16.Nf2+

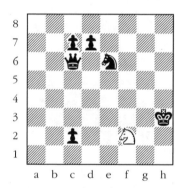

#97

1.Nc7 2.Ne6 3.Nf4 4.Ng6 5.Nxh8

6.Ng6 7.Nf4 8.Nh5 9.Ng3 10.Nxh1 11.Ng3 12.Nf5 13.Nxd4 14.Nxc2 15.Nd4 16.Nxc6+

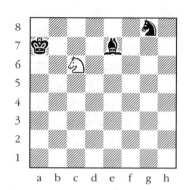

#98

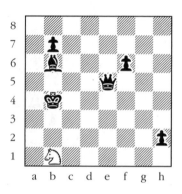

1.Nd2 2.Nf3 3.Nh4 4.Ng6 5.Nf8 6.Nd7 7.Nxb6 8.Nd7 9.Nf8 10.Ng6 11.Nh8 12.Nf7 13.Nh6 14.Ng4 15.Nf2 16.Nd3+

#99

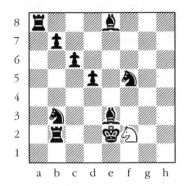

1.Ng4 2.Nf6 3.Nh7 4.Nf8 5.Ne6
6.Nc7 7.Nxa8 8.Nc7 9.Nxe8 10.Nc7
11.Ne6 12.Nd8 13.Nxb7 14.Nd8
15.Nxc6 16.Nb4 17.Nxd5 18.Nc3+

#100

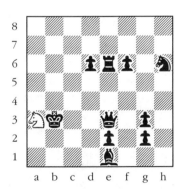

1.Nb5 2.Nc7 3.Na6 4.Nb8 5.Nd7

6.Nf8 7.Ng6 8.Nh4 9.Nxg2 10.Nxe1
11.Ng2 12.Nh4 13.Ng6 14.Nf8 15.Nd7
16.Nb8 17.Nc6 18.Na5+

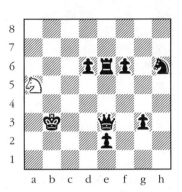

#101

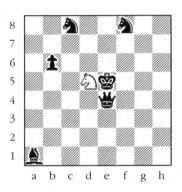

1.Nc7 2.Ne8 3.Ng7 4.Nh5 5.Ng3
6.Nf1 7.Nd2 8.Nb3 9.Nxa1 10.Nb3
11.Nc1 12.Na2 13.Nc3 14.Nd1 15.Nf2
16.Nh3 17.Ng5 18.Nf7+

95

#102

1.Ng6 2.Nh4 3.Nf3 4.Ng1 5.Nh3
6.Nf2 7.Nxd3 8.Nf2 9.Nh3 10.Ng1

11.Nf3 12.Nd2 13.Nc4 14.Nb6
15.Nxa8 16.Nb6 17.Nc4 18.Nxa3
19.Nc4 20.Nd2 21.Nf3 22.Nh4 23.Ng6
24.Nf8+

Solutions: Queen Mazes

#103

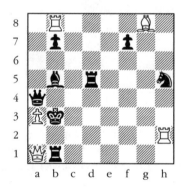

1.Qh8 2.Qh7 3.Qxf7 4.Qxb7
5.Qh7 6.Qd3#. Both rook and bishop
are pinned to the king and neither may
take at d3.

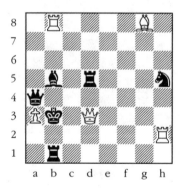

#104

1.Qxb5 2.Qxd8 3.Qbxb8 4.Qg3 5.Qd3#. We couldn't decide which one was the maze queen and which one was the helper, so we ended up using both.

#105

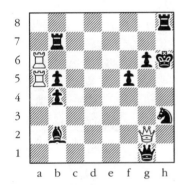

1.Qxb7 2.Qxb5 3.Qxf5 4.Qc2 5.Qxb2 6.Qxh8#

#106

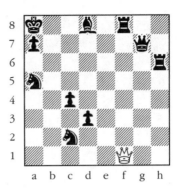

1.Qb1 2.Qa2 3.Qa4 4.Qb5 5.Qc5 6.Qc8#

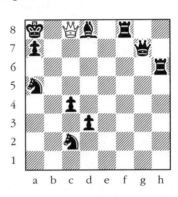

#107

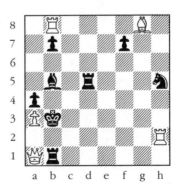

1.Qh8 2.Qh6 3.Qb6 4.Qa5 5.Qb4#

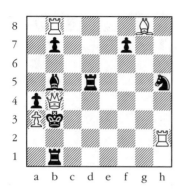

#108

1.Qb4 2.Qb1 3.Qh7 4.Qxh4 5.Qe1 6.Qh1 7.Qh2 8.Qc7#

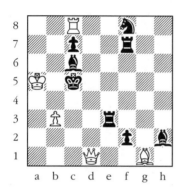

1.Qg4 2.Qg8 3.Qxf7 4.Qxf2 5.Qxh2 6.Qxc7 7.Qe5#

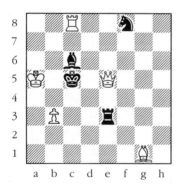

#110

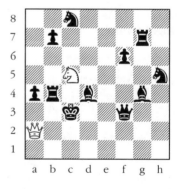

1.Qh2 2.Qb8 3.Qa8 4.Qa5 5.Qd8 6.Qh8 7.Qh6 8.Qc1#

#112

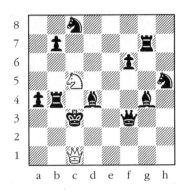

#111

1.Qc6 2.Qa4 3.Qa1 4.Qxf6 5.Qxd6
6.Qxc7 7.Qxb8 8.Qxb1 9.Qh7#

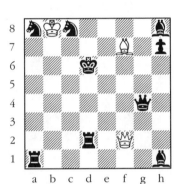

1.Qe3 2.Qe8 3.Qxh8 4.Qxa1
5.Qxh1 6.Qxa8 7.Qb7 8.Qc7#

#113

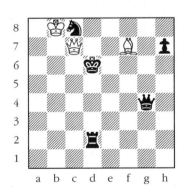

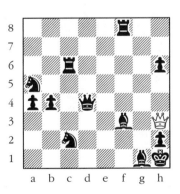

1.Qf1 2.Qb1 3.Qa2 4.Qxa4 5.Qxa5
6.Qb5 7.Qb7 8.Qe7 9.Qxf8 10. Qxf3#

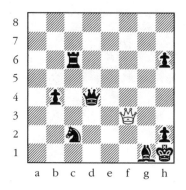

#114

1.Qxa1 2.Qxh8 3.Qxh4 4.Qxe1
5.Qxe7 6.Qxd7 7.Qxa4 8.Qxb3
9.Qxf3#

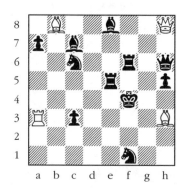

1.Qg8 2.Qb3 3.Qb7 4.Qxc7 5.Qb7
6.Qb3 7.Qxc3 8.Qe1 9.Qh4#

#116

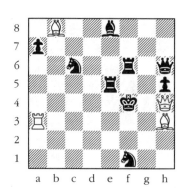

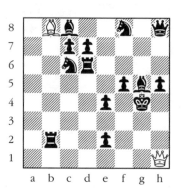

1.Qa1 2.Qa4 3.Qc4 4.Qf7 5.Qe8
6.Qxc8 7.Qxc7 8.Qxd6 9.Qg3#

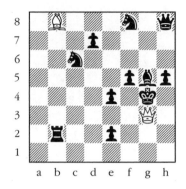

#118

#117

1.Qg3 2.Qh4 3.Qh5 4.Qf5 5.Qd3
6.Qe3 7.Qe8 8.Qa4 9.Qa1#

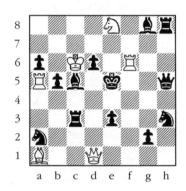

1.Qb1 2.Qb2 3.Qxg2 4.Qg7 5.Qb7
6.Qxa6 7.Qxb5 8. Qd3 9.Qxe3#

#119

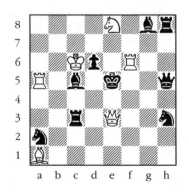

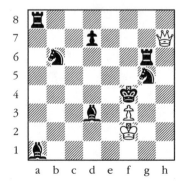

1.Qh1 2.Qd1 3.Qxd3 4.Qxg6
5.Qxb6 6.Qb7 7.Qxa8 8.Qxa1 9.Qf6#

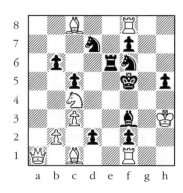

#121

#120

1.Qa7 2.Qc7 3.Qg3 4.Qg7 5.Qxf7 6.Qxd7 7.Qxd2 8.Qxf2 9.Qc2#

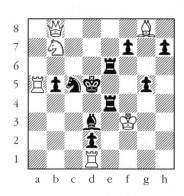

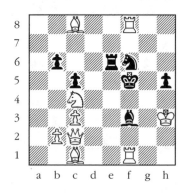

1.Qh2 2.Qxd2 3.Qb2 4.Qxb5 5.Qb2 6.Qg7 7.Qxf7 8.Qxh7 9.Qxe4#

#122

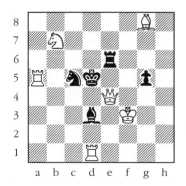

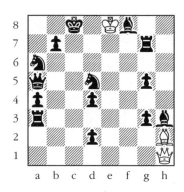

1.Qd1 2.Qh5 3.Qh8 4.Qxf8 5.Qxa3 6.Qf8 7.Qxg7 8.Qxg5 9.Qxg3 10.Qxh3#

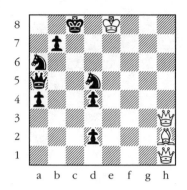

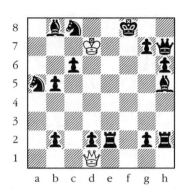

#123

1.Qg1 2.Qd4 3.Qc3 4.Qxa5 5.Qa8
6.Qxb8 7.Qxh2 8.Qxh5 9.Qxe2
10.Qe8#

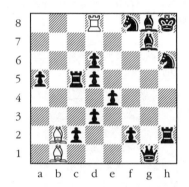

1.Qa4 2.Qe8 3.Qxf8 4.Qxd6
5.Qxc5 6.Qxd5 7.Qxe4 8.Qxd3
9.Qxc2 10.Qh7#

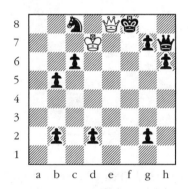

#125

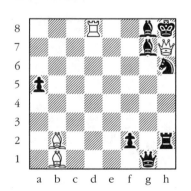

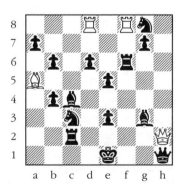

1.Qxc2 2.Qb2 3.Qxb4 4.Qxc4
5.Qxg8 6.Qxg7 7.Qxf6 8.Qxd6 9.Qd3
10.Qxe3#

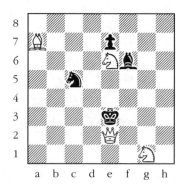

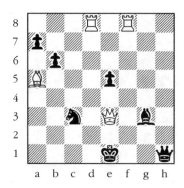

#126

1.Qg6 2.Qf5 3.Qd5 4.Qc6 5.Qc7
6.Qxh2 7.Qxb8 8.Qxb6 9.Qxa6
10.Qe2#

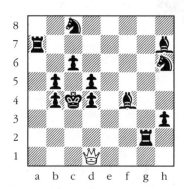

1.Qh5 2.Qxh3 3.Qxg2 4.Qh3
5.Qxc8 6.Qd8 7.Qb6 8.Qxa7 9.Qxh7
10.Qc2#

#128

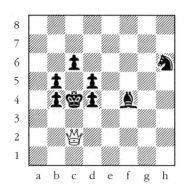

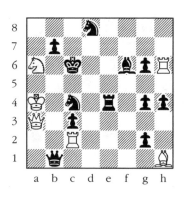

1.Qf8 2.Qg8 3.Qxg6 4.Qg8
5.Qxd8 6.Qd3 7.Qxc3 8.Qd2 9.Qxg2

10.Qxg4 11.Qe6#

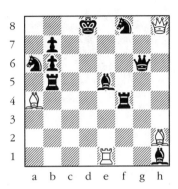

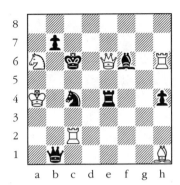

#129

**1.Qh3 2.Qe3 3.Qe2 4.Qxb5
5.Qxe5 6.Qxf4 7.Qf1 8.Qxh1 9.Qxb7
10.Qxa6 11.Qa8#**

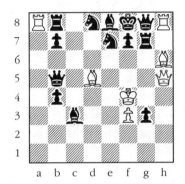

**1.Qh1 2.Qg1 3.Qa7 4.Qxb8
5.Qxd8 6.Qb8 7.Qa7 8.Qg1 9.Qh1
10.Qh5 11.Qxf7#**

#131

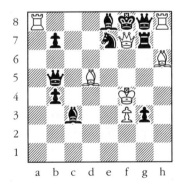

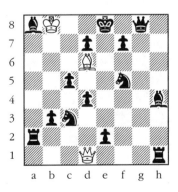

**1.Qd3 2.Qxf5 3.Qxc5 4.Qxd4
5.Qxc3 6.Qxb3 7.Qxa2 8.Qxa8**

9.Qxh1 10.Qxh4 11.Qe7#

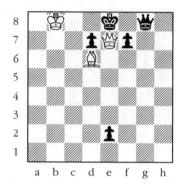

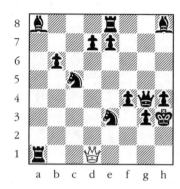

#132

1.Qa3 2.Qxg3 2.Qa3 4.Qxf8 5.Qf1 6.Qb5 7.Qxd7 8.Qxg7 9.Qxa7 10.Qxg1 11.Qd1#

1.Qd2 2.Qb4 3.Qxb6 4.Qh6 5.Qh7 6.Qf7 7.Qxe8 8.Qxh8 9.Qxa1 10.Qxa8 11.Qh1#

#134

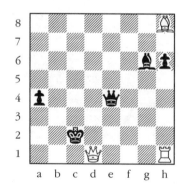

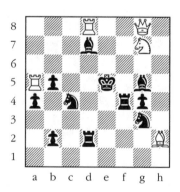

1.Qh7 2.Qb1 3.Qg1 4.Qxg3 5.Qg1 6.Qf1 7.Qxc4 8.Qb4 9.Qxd2 10.Qxd7

11.Qd4#

#136

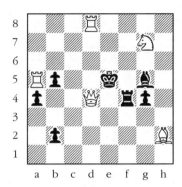

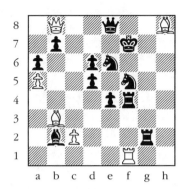

#135

1.Qa7 2.Qb6 3.Qb4 4.Qe1 5.Qd1
6.Qxd5 7.Qd1 8.Qb1 9.Qxb2 10.Qc1
11.Qxf4 12.Qxe4 13.Qxg2 14.Qg7#

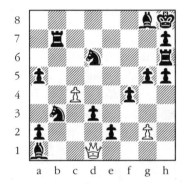

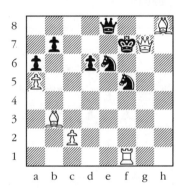

1.Qxd3 2.Qf3 3.Qc6 4.Qa6 5.Qa8
6.Qf8 7.Qxh6 8.Qxd6 9.Qc6[a6]
10.Qxb7 11.Qxb3 12.Qxa2 13.Qxa1#

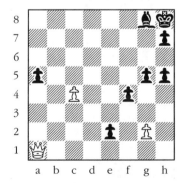

Solutions: Pawn Mazes

#137

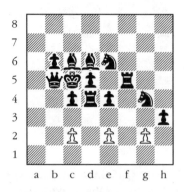

1.gxh3 2.hxg4 3.gxf5 4.fxe6 5.e3
6.c3 7.exd4#

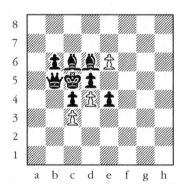

#138

1.cxd3 2.dxe4 3.exf5 4.fxg6 5.h4
6.h5 7.h6 8.g7#

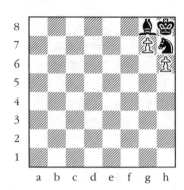

#139

1.hxg4 2.gxf5 3.c4 4.c5 5.cxd6
6.fxg6 7.g7 8.gxh8=Q#

#140

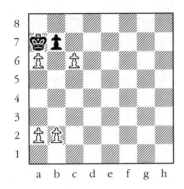

1.axb7 2.b4 3.b5 4.a4 5.a5 6.a6 7.c7 8.b8=Q#

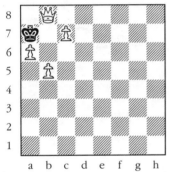

#141

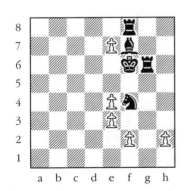

1.exf8=Q 2.exf4 3.f5 4.h4 5.h5 6.hxg6 7.g7 8.f4 9.g8=N#

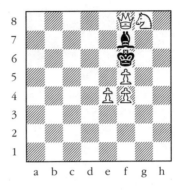

#142

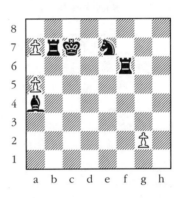

1.a8=Q 2.g4 3.g5 4.gxf6 5.f7 6.f8=N 7.a6 8.axb7 9.b8=Q#

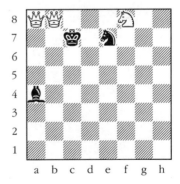

#143

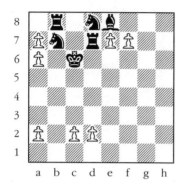

**1.fxe8=Q 2.axb8=Q 3.a7 4.a8=Q
5.a4 6.a5 7.c4 8.d4 9.exd8=N#**

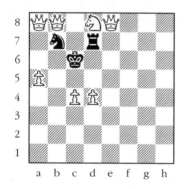

#144

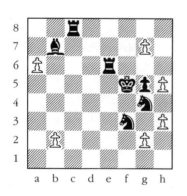

**1.axb7 2.bxc8=Q 3.b4 4.b5 5.b6
6.b7 7.b8=Q 8.g8=N 9.gxf3 10.hxg4#**

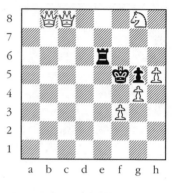

#145

**1.fxg4 2.c4 3.c5 4.cxd6 5.dxe7 6.g5
7.h4 8.h5 9.h6 10.exf8=N#**

#146

1.cxd5 2.dxe6 3.d4 4.d5 5.fxg6
6.g7 7.g8=Q 8.e4 9.e5 10.d6#

#148

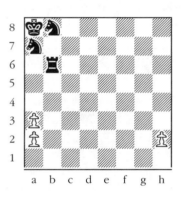

#147

1.a4 2.a5 3.axb6 4.h4 5.h5 6.h6
7.h7 8.h8=Q 9.a4 10.a5 11.a6 12.b7#

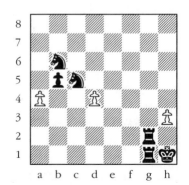

1.a5 2.dxc5 3.cxb6 4.a6 5.a7
6.a8=Q 7.h4 8.h5 9.h6 10.h7
11.h8=Q#

#149

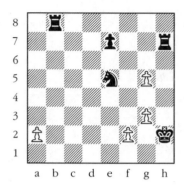

1.a4 2.a5 3.a6 4.a7 5.axb8=Q 6.g4
7.g6 8.gxh7 9.g5 10.g6 11.g7 12.g8=Q
13.h8=Q#

#150

1.b8=Q 2.axb6 3.bxa7 4.a8=Q 5.f7
6.f8=Q 7.d4 8.d5 9.d6 10.d7 11.d8=Q

12.h3 13.g3#

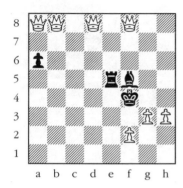

#151

1.hxg5 2.d3 3.dxe4 4.e5 5.e6 6.e7
7.e8=Q 8.g6 9.g4 10.g5 11.f4 12.f5
13.f6#

#152

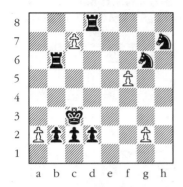

1.cxd8=Q 2.a4 3.a5 4.axb6 5.b7
6.b8=Q 7.fxg6 8.gxh7 9.g4 10.g5
11.g6 12.g7 13.g8=Q 14.h8=Q#

#153

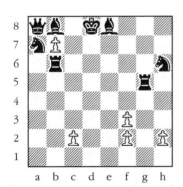

Our solution ran: **1.bxa8=Q 2.h4
3.hxg5 4.c4 5.c5 6.cxb6 7.bxa7 8.gxh6**

9.h7 10.h8=Q 11.f4 12.f5 13.f6 14.f7
15.f8=N 16.f4 17.f5 18.f6 19.axb8=Q#

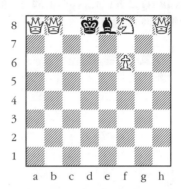

Then a clever student found a shorter
solution: **1.bxa8=Q 2.h4 3.hxg5 4.c4
5.c5 6.cxb6 7.bxa7 8.axb8=B** (The joy
of underpromotion!)

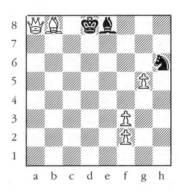

**9.gxh6 10.h7 11.h8=Q 12.f4 13.f5
14.f6 15.f7 16.fxe8=Q#**

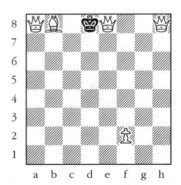

Adding insult to injury, a still shorter solution was soon discovered: **1.bxa8=Q 2.h4 3.hxg5 4.c4 5.c5 6.cxb6** (the pawn stays here)

7.gxh6 8.h7 9.h8=Q 10.f4 11.f5 12.f6 13.f7 14.fxe8=Q#

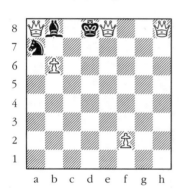

Tricky devils, these pawn mazes.

#154

1.gxf4 2.fxe5 3.exd6 4.dxc7 5.cxb8=Q 6.f4 7.f5 8.f6 9.f7 10.f8=Q 11.g4 12.g5 13.g6 14.g7 15.g8=Q#

#155

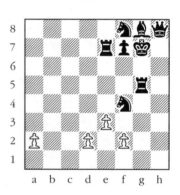

1.exf4 2.fxg5 3.d4 4.d5 5.d6 6.dxe7 7.a4 8.a5 9.a6 10.a7 11.a8=Q 12.exf8=N 13.f4 14.f5 15.f6#

114

#156

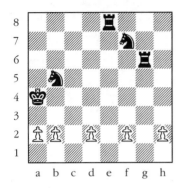

1.h4 2.h5 3.hxg6 4.gxf7 5.fxe8=Q
6.f4 7.f5 8.f6 9.f7 10.f8=Q 11.d4 12.d5
13.d6 14.d7 15.d8=Q 16.b3#

#157

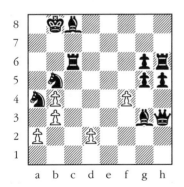

1.fxg5 2.gxh6 3.h7 4.h8=Q 5.bxa4
6.axb5 7.d4 8.d5 9.dxc6 10.b6 11.b7

12.b5 13.b6 14.a4 15.a5 16.a6 17.a7#

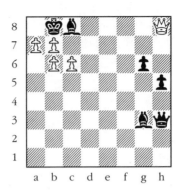

#158

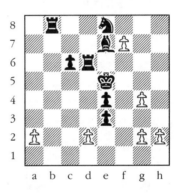

1.dxe3 2.a4 3.a5 4.a6 5.a7
6.axb8=Q 7.fxe8=Q 8.g5 9.g6 10.g7
11.g8=Q 12.g4 13.h4 14.h5 15.h6
16.h7 17.h8=Q#

#159

**1.bxa3 2.axb4 3.g7 4.gxf8=N
5.exf3 6.f4 7.f5 8.f6 9.b5 10.b6 11.b7
12.axb3 13.b4 14.b5 15.c4 16.d4
17.b8=Q#**

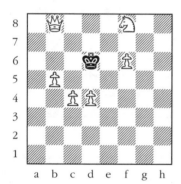

#160

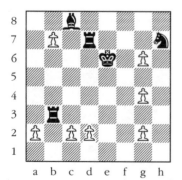

**1.bxc8=Q 2.axb3 3.b4 4.b5 5.b6
6.b7 7.b8=Q 8.c4 9.d4 10.gxh7 11.g5
12.g6 13.g7 14.g8=N 15.g4 16.h8=N
17.d5#**

Capturing with the c-pawn at move
two extends the solution to 21 moves:
**1.bxc8=Q 2.cxb3 3.gxh7 4.a4 5.a5
6.a7 8.a8=Q 9.b4 10.b5 11.b6 12.b7
13.b8=Q 14.h8=N 15.g5 16.g6 17.g7
18.g8=N 19.g4 20.d4 21.d5#**. And yes,
this was the originally intended solution.

#161

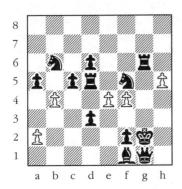

1.bxa5 2.axb6 3.a4 4.a5 5.a6 6.a7 7.a8=Q 8.exf5 9.fxg6 10.f5 11.f6 12.f7 13.f8=Q 14.h6 15.h7 16.h8=Q 17.g7 18.g8=Q#

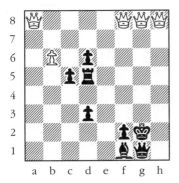

#162

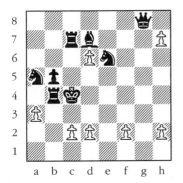

1.hxg8=Q 2.h4 3.h5 4.h6 5.h7 6.h8=Q 7.f4 8.f5 9.f6 10.f7 11.f8=Q 12.dxc7 The advance of the h-pawn could have waited. But the f-pawn must queen before White takes at c7. If dxc7 is played prematurely, then f6-f7 can be answered by ...Nxc7 since the knight is unpinned. **13.axb4 14.bxa5 15.a6 16.a7 17.a8=Q 18.d3#**

#163

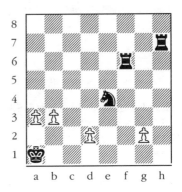

1.d3 2.dxe4 3.e5 4.exf6 5.g4 6.g5 7.g6 8.gxh7 9.b4 10.b5 11.b6 12.b7 13.b8=Q 14.a4 15.a5 16.a6 17.a7 18.a8=Q#

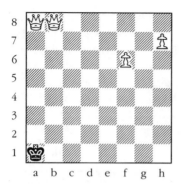

White can vary his move order somewhat, but the black rooks must be eliminated before White's a- and b-pawns cross the 6th and 7th ranks.

#164

1.hxg3 2.gxf4 3.d4 4.dxe5 5.b4 6.bxa5 7.a6 8.a7 9.a8=Q 10.a4 11.a5 12.f5 13.f6 14.f7 15.f8=N 16.e6 17.e7 18.e8=N#

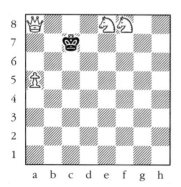

White could also have made queens at e8 and f8, then mated with a knight on a8, but it takes one move longer as the a-pawn must travel to a6: **1.hxg3 2.gxf4 3.d4 4.dxe5 5.e6 6.e7 7.e8=Q 8.f5 9.f6 10.f7 11.f8=Q 12.b4 13.bxa5 14.a6 15.a7 16.a4 17.a5 18.a6 19.a8=N#**

Here's a cautionary note for those who want to construct their own mazes: Watch out for duals! A minor dual is tolerable and we've let some pass, but a major dual wrecks the problem. Here's what happened with an early version of #164:

Early Version #164

1.hxg3 2.gxf4 3.fxe5 4.b4 5.bxa5 6.a6 7.a7 8.a8=Q 9.a4 10.a5 11.c4 12.c5 13.c6 14.e6 15.e7 16.e8=N#

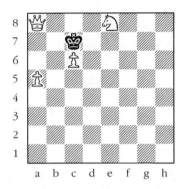

Looks fine until you spot the symmetry: **1.hxg3 2.gxf4 3.fxe5 4.b4 5.bxa5 6.e6 7.e7 8.e8=Q 9.c4 10.c5 11.a6 12.a7 13.a4 14.a5 15.a6 16.a8=N#**

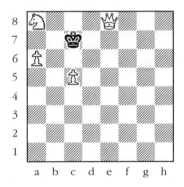

#165

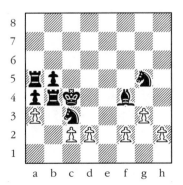

1.gxf4 2.fxg5 3.h4 4.h5 5.h6 6.h7 7.h8=Q 8.f4 9.f5 10.f6 11.f7 12.f8=Q 13.axb4 14.bxa5 15.a6 16.a7 17.a8=Q 18.d3#. The c3-knight is a red herring; don't touch it. Also, don't try to queen the g-pawn.

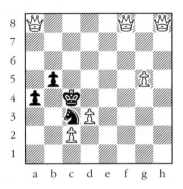

#166

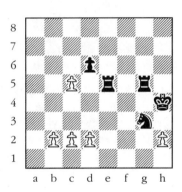

1.cxd6 2.2.d7 3.d8=Q 4.d4 5.dxe5 6.e6 7.e7 8.e8=Q 9.c4 10.c5 11.c6 12.c7 13.c8=Q 14.b4 15.b5 16.b6 17.b7 18.b8=Q 19.hxg3#

#167

#168

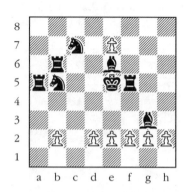

1.fxg3 2.b4 3.bxa5 4.axb6 5.b7 6.b8=Q 7.e8=Q 8.d3 9.e4 10.g4 11.gxf5 12.g4 13.g5 14.f6 15.f7 16.f8=Q 17.h4 18.h5 19.h6 20.h7 21.h8=Q#

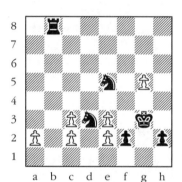

1.a4 2.a5 3.a6 4.a7 5.a8=Q 6.cxd3 7.d4 (It is simplest to advance the d-pawn first. If 7.c4 8.c5 9.c6 White must still play 10.d4, because 10.c7? unpins the knight allowing ...Nxd3. Leaving pawns *en prise* is the same as putting pawns *en prise*. It's a no-no) **8.d5 9.d6 10.d7 11.d8=Q 12.c4 13.c5 14.c6 15.c7 16.c8=Q 17.g6 18.g7 19.g8=Q#**

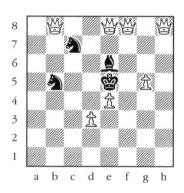

#169

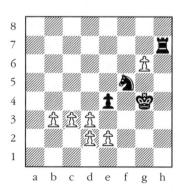

1.dxe4 2.gxh7 3.h8=Q 4.b4 5.b5
6.b6 7.b7 8.b8=Q 9.c4 10 c5 11.c6
12.c7 13.c8=Q 14.exf5 15.e4 16.d4
17.d5 18.d6 19.d7 20.f6 21.f7 22.f8=Q
23.d8=Q#

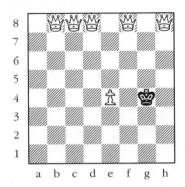

This is a replacement #169. The
original fooled us and was banished to
the back of the book.

Original #169

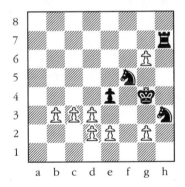

The intended solution ran: **1.dxe4
2.gxh7 3.h8=Q 4.c4 5.c5 6.c6 7.c7
8.c8=Q 9.exf5 10.e4** Since White is not
allowed to give check, he must arrange
to block the c8-h3 diagonal so that his
f-pawn and later his d-pawn can advance.

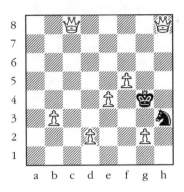

**11.d4 12.d5 13.d6 14.d7 15.f6 16.f7
17.f8=Q 18.e5 19.e6 20.d8=Q 21.b4
22.b5 23.b6 24.b7 25.b8=Q** (naturally
the b-pawn could have advanced ear-
lier) **26.gxh3#**

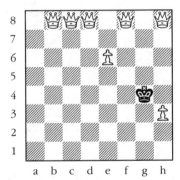

Then we discovered (on our own —
no help from smart students) that by not
taking the f5-knight the solution can be
shortened: **1.dxe4 2.gxh7 3.h8=Q 4.c4
5.c5 6.c6 7.c7 8.c8=Q 9.b4 10.b5 11.b6
12.b7 13.b8=Q 14.d4 15.d5 16.d6
17.d7 18.d8=Q 19.hxg3#**

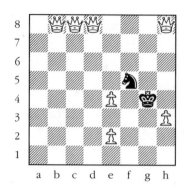

1.gxf5 2.f4 3.fxg5 4.g6 5.gxh7
6.h8=Q 7.f6 8.f7 9.f8=Q 10.g4 11.g5
12.g6 13.g7 14.g8=Q 15.b7 16.b8=Q
17.d4 18.d5 19.d6 20.d7 21.d8=Q
22.b3 23.a4 24.a5 25.a6 26.a7
27.a8=Q 28.c3#

Tricky little devils, these pawn mazes.

#170

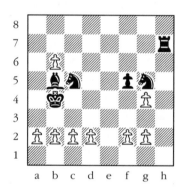

Promotion of the h- and g-pawns can be delayed. However, both the f- and b-pawns must promote before the d-pawn can advance. And the d-pawn must promote to allow the a-pawn to reach a5.

Solutions: King Mazes

#171

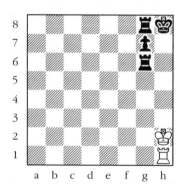

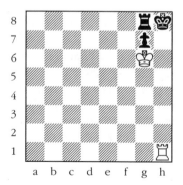

1.Kh3 2.Kh4 3.Kh5 4.Kxg6#

122

#172

1.Kf3 2.Ke4 3.Kd5 4.Kc6 5.Kc7#

#173

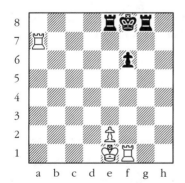

1.Kf2 2.Kf3 3.Kf4 4.Kf5 5.Kxf6
6.Kf5 7.Kf4 8.Kf3 9.Kf2 10.Ke1#

#174

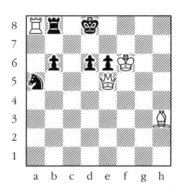

1.Kxe6 2.Kxd6 3.Kd5 4.Kd4
5.Kc3 6.Kb4 7.Kb5 8.Ka6 9.Ka7
10.Kxb8 11.Ka7#

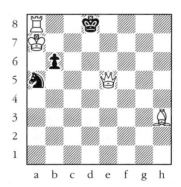

#175

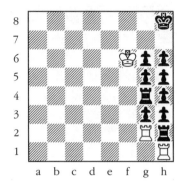

1.Kxg6 2.Kxh6 3.Kxh5 4.Kxg4
5.Kxg5 6.Kxh4 7.Kxg3 8.Kxh2
9.Kxh3 10.Kh2 11.Kg1#

#176

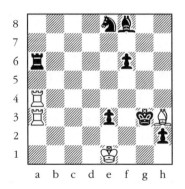

1.Ke2 2.Kd3 3.Ke4 4.Kf5 5.Kg6
6.Kf7 7.Kxf8 8.Kf7 9.Kg6 10.Kf5

11.Ke4 12.Kxe3 13.Ke2#

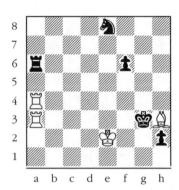

#177

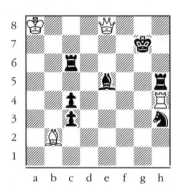

1.Kb7 2.Kxc6 3.Kd5 4.Ke4 5.Kf3
6.Kg4 7.Kxh5 8.Kg4 9.Kf5 10.Kxe5
11.Kd4 12.Kxc3 13.Kxc4#

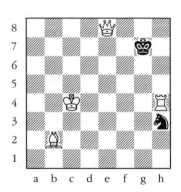

124

#178

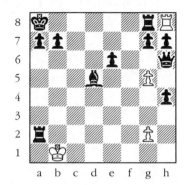

1.Kc1 2.Kd1 3.Ke1 4.Kf1 5.Kg1
6.Kh2 7.Kh3 8.Kg4 9.Kf4 10.Ke5
11.Kd6 12.Ke7 13.Kf7 14.Kxg8
15.Kf7#

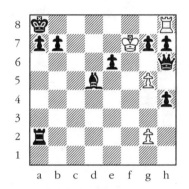

#179

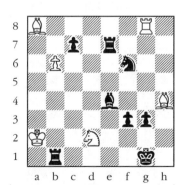

1.Ka3 2.Ka4 3.Ka5 4.Ka6 5.Ka7

6.Kb8 7.Kc8 8.Kd8 9.Kxe7 10.Kxf6
11.Ke5 12.Kxe4 13.Kxf3 14.Kxg3
15.Kh3#

#180

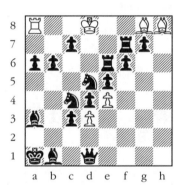

1.Kc8 2.Kb7 3.Kxa6 4.Kb5
5.Kxc4 6.Kxd5 7.Kxe6 8.Kxf7
9.Kxg7 10.Kxf6 11.Kxe5 12.Kxd4
13.Kxc3 14.Kd4 15.Ke3#

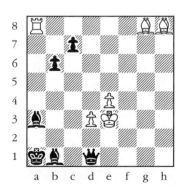

125

#181

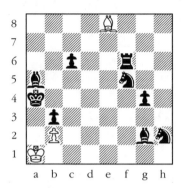

1.Kb1 2.Kc1 3.Kd1 4.Ke2 5.Kf2
6.Kxg2 7.Kf2 8.Ke2 9.Kd3 10.Ke4
11.Ke5 12.Kxf6 13.Ke6 14.Kd7
15.Kxc6 16.Kc5#

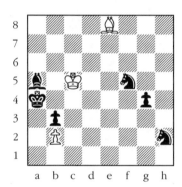

#182

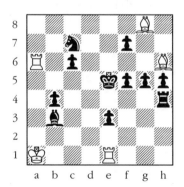

1.Kb2 2.Kxb3 3.Ka4 4.Ka5 5.Kb6

6.Kxc6 7.Kd7 8.Ke7 9.Kxf7 10.Kg6
11.Kxg5 12.Kxh4 13.Kg3 14.Kf3
15.Kxe3 16.Kd3#

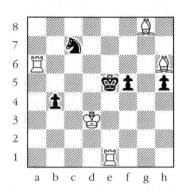

#183

1.Kc4 2.Kd5 3.Ke6 4.Kf7 5.Kg8
6.Kxh8 7.Kg8 8.Kf7 9.Ke6 10.Kd5
11.Kc4 12.Kb3 13.Kxa2 14.Ka3
15.Ka4 16.Kb5#

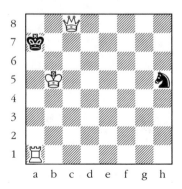

126

#184

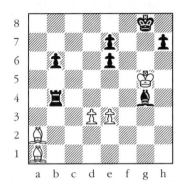

1.Kh4 2.Kg3 3.Kf2 4.Ke1 5.Kd2
6.Kc3 7.Kxb4 8.Kc4 9.Kd4 10.Ke4
11.Kf4 12.Kxg4 13.Kf4 14.Ke5
15.Kxe6 16.Kxe7#

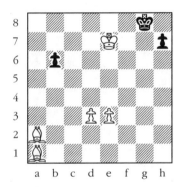

#185

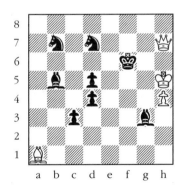

1.Kg4 2.Kxg3 3.Kf2 4.Ke1 5.Kd1

6.Kc2 7.Kb3 8.Kb4 9.Kxb5 10.Kc6
11.Kxd7 12.Kc6 13.Kxd5 14.Kxd4
15.Kxc3 16.Kd4 17.Kd5#

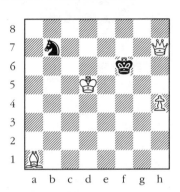

#186

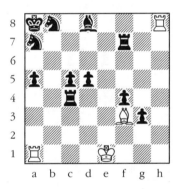

1.Kf1 2.Kg2 3.Kh3 4.Kg4 5.Kh5
6.Kg6 7.Kxf7 8.Ke8 9.Kxd8 10.Kc7
11.Kb6 12.Kxa5 13.Kb6 14.Kc7
15.Kd6 16.Kxd5 17.Kxc4#

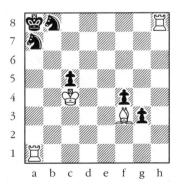

127

#187

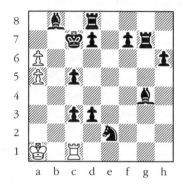

1.Ka2 2.Kb3 3.Kc4 4.Kxd3 5.Ke4
6.Ke5 7.Kf6 8.Kxg7 9.Kxh6 10.Kg5
11.Kxg4 12.Kf3 13.Kxe2 14.Kd3
15.Kxc3 16.Kc4 17.Kxc5 18.Kd5#

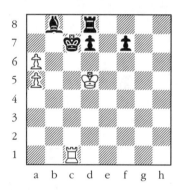

#188

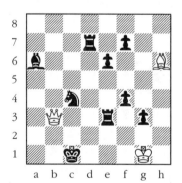

1.Kg2 2.Kh3 3.Kg4 4.Kxf4 5.Kg5
6.Kf6 7.Kg7 8.Kf8 9.Ke8 10.Kxd7
11.Kc7 12.Kb8 13.Ka7 14.Kxa6
15.Kb5 16.Kxc4 17.Kd4 18.Kxe3
19.Ke2#

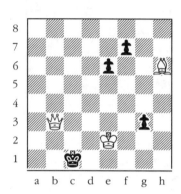

#189

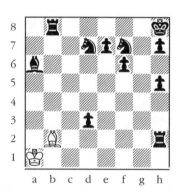

1.Kb1 2.Kc1 3.Kd1 4.Ke1 5.Kf1
6.Kg1 7.Kxh2 8.Kg3 9.Kf4 10.Kf5
11.Ke6 12.Kxd7 13.Kc7 14.Kxb8
15.Kc7 16.Kd7 17.Kxe7 18.Kxf6
19.Kxf7#

#191

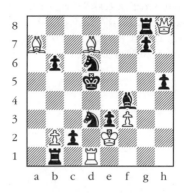

1.Kf1 2.Kg2 3.Kh3 4.Kh4 5.Kxh5
6.Kg6 7.Kh7 8.Kxg8 9.Kxg7 10.Kf8
11.Ke7 12.Kd8 13.Kc7 14.Kxb6
15.Ka5 16.Ka4 17.Kb3 18.Kxc2
19.Kxb1 20.Kc2 21.Kxd3 22.Kc3#

#190

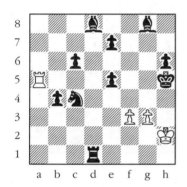

1.Kg2 2.Kf2 3.Ke2 4.Kxd1 5.Kc2
6.Kb3 7.Kxb4 8.Kc5 9.Kxc6 10.Kd7
11.Kxd8 12.Kxe7 13.Kf8 14.Kxg8
15.Kf7 16.Ke6 17.Kd5 18.Kxc4
19.Kd5 20.Kxe5 21.Kf6#

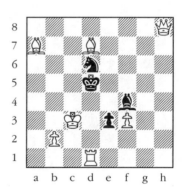

#192

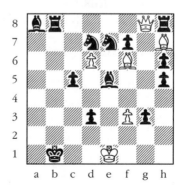

1.Kf1 2.Kg2 3.Kh3 4.Kh4 5.Kxh5
6.Kxh6 7.Kg7 8.Kxh8 9.Kg7 10.Kxf7
11.Kxe7 12.Kxd7 13.Kc7 14.Kxb8
15.Kxa8 16.Kb7 17.Kc6 18.Kd5
19.Kxe5 20.Ke4 21.Kxd3 22.Kd2#

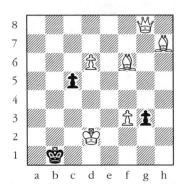

#193

#194

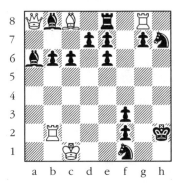

1.Kg8 2.Kf8 3.Ke8 4.Kd8 5.Kc8
6.Kxb7 7.Kc8 8.Kd8 9.Ke8 10.Kf8
11.Kg8 12.Kh7 13.Kh6 14.Kh5
15.Kh4 16.Kh3 17.Kh2 18.Kxg1
19.Kf1 20.Ke1 21.Kd1 22.Kc2#

1 Kc2 2.Kc3 3.Kd4 4.Ke4 5.Kxf3
6.Kg4 7.Kh5 8.Kg6 9.Kxg7 10.Kf7
11.Kxe8 12.Kxd7 13.Kxe6 14.Kd7
15.Kxc6 16.Kxb6 17.Kxa6 18.Kb5
19.Kc4 20.Kd3 21.Ke2 22.Kxf2
23.Kxf1#

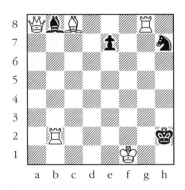

#195

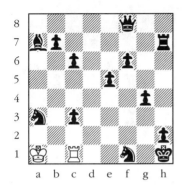

1.Ka2 2.Kb3 3.Kxc3 4.Kd3 5.Ke4
6.Kf5 7.Kg6 8.Kxh7 9.Kg6 10.Kf5
11.Ke6 12.Kd7 13.Kc7 14.Kxb7
15.Kxa7 16.Kb6[b7] 17.Kxc6 18.Kd5
19.Ke4 20.Kd3 21.Ke2 22.Kxf1
23.Kf2#

1.Kg2 2.Kf3 3.Kg4 4.Kf5 5.Kg6
6.Kxh7 7.Kg6 8.Kxf6 9.Ke7 10.Kxd6
11.Kxe5 12.Kd4 13.Kxc4 14.Kb5
15.Kxa5 16.Kb5 17.Kc4 18.Kd4
19.Ke5 20.Kf4 21.Kxg3 22.Kf3
23.Kxe2#

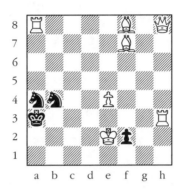

#197

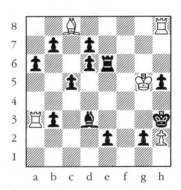

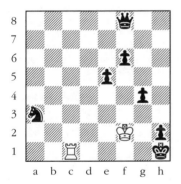

#196

1.Kf4 2.Kf3 3.Kf2 4.Ke1 5.Kd2
6.Kc3 7.Kxb3 8.Ka4 9.Ka5 10.Kb6
11.Kc7 12.Kxd7 13.Kc7 14.Kb6
15.Ka5 16.Ka4 17.Kb3 18.Kc3
19.Kd2 20.Ke1 21.Kf2 22.Kf3 23.Kf4
23.Kg5 25.Kxh5 26.Kg5#

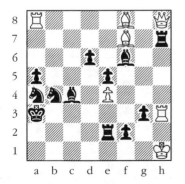

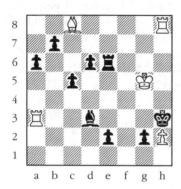

#198

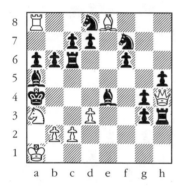

1.Kb1 2.Kc1 3.Kd1 4.Ke2 5.Ke3
6.Kxe4 7.Kf5 8.Kg6 9.Kg7 10.Kf8
11.Ke7 12.Kxd7 13.Kc8 14.Kb8
15.Ka7 16.Kxa6 17.Ka7 18.Kb8
19.Kc8 20.Kd7 21.Ke7 22.Kf8
23.Kg7 24.Kg6 25.Kxh5 26.Kxg4
27.Kxh3#

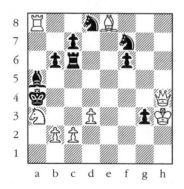

#199

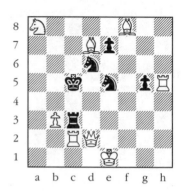

1.Kd1 2.Kc1 3.Kb2 4.Ka3 5.Ka4
6.Ka5 7.Ka6 8.Ka7 9.Kb8 10.Kc7
11.Kd8 12.Kxe7 13.Kf6 14.Kxg5
15.Kf6 16.Ke7 17.Kd8 18.Kc7 19.Kb8
20.Ka7 21.Ka6 22.Ka5 23.Ka4 24.Ka3
25.Kb2 26.Kxc3 27.Kb2#

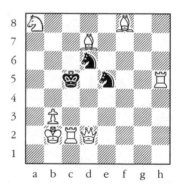

#200

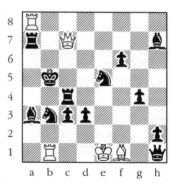

1.Kf2 2.Kg3 3.Kh4 4.Kh5 5.Kh6
6.Kxh7 7.Kg7 8.Kxf6 9.Kxe5 10.Ke6
11.Kd7 12.Kc8 13.Kb8 14.Kxa7
15.Kb8 16.Kc8 17.Kd7 18.Ke6
19.Kf5[f6] 20.Kg5 21.Kh4 22.Kg3
23.Kf2 24.Ke3 25.Kxd3 26.Kc2
27.Kxb3 28.Kxa3#

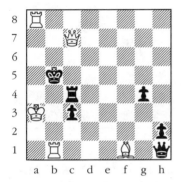

#201

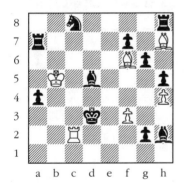

1.Kb4 2.Ka3 3.Kb2 4.Kc1 5.Kd1
6.Ke1 7.Kf2 8.Kxg2 9.Kxh2 10.Kg3
11.Kf4 12.Kg5 13.Kh6 14.Kg7
15.Kxh8 16.Kg8[g7] You're half way
there.

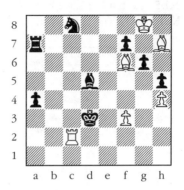

17.Kf8 18.Ke8 19.Kd8 20.Kxc8
21.Kb8 22.Kxa7 23.Kb6 24.Kc5
25.Kxd5 26.Kd6 27.Ke7 28.Kxf7
29.Kxg6 30.Kf5 31.Kf4#

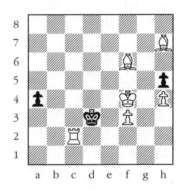

#202

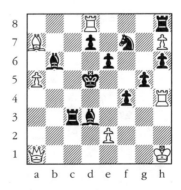

1.Kg2 2.Kf1 3.Ke1 4.Kd2 5.Kxc3
6.Kxd3 7.Kc3 8.Kb4 9.Kb5 10.Kxb6

11.Kb5 12.Kb4 13.Kc3 14.Kd2 15.Ke1 16.Kf2 The halfway mark.

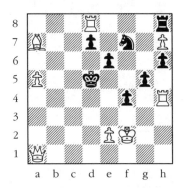

17.Kf3 18.Kg4 19.Kh5 20.Kg6 21.Kxf7 22.Kg7 23.Kxh8 24.Kg7 25.Kxh6 26.Kxg5 27.Kxf4 28.Kg5 29.Kf6 30.Ke7 31.Kxd7 32.Kc7#

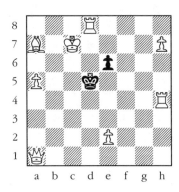

#203

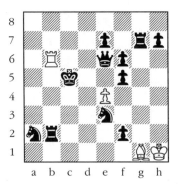

1.Kh2 2.Kh3 3.Kh4 4.Kh5 5.Kh6 6.Kxg7 7.Kf8 8.Ke8 9.Kd8 10.Kc7 11.Kb7 12.Ka6 13.Ka5 14.Ka4 15.Ka3 16.Kxb2 17.Ka3 The international date line has been crossed.

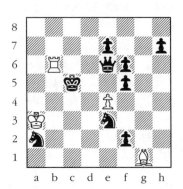

18.Ka4 19.Ka5 20.Ka6 21.Kb7 22.Kc7 23.Kd8 24.Ke8 25.Kf8 26.Kg7 27.Kh6 28.Kh5 29.Kh4 30.Kg3 31.Kxf2 32.Kxe3 33.Kd3#

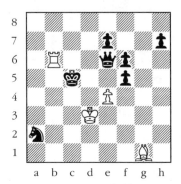

#203 discussion: The alternative after taking the first black rook, 6.Kxg7, is for White to return clockwise and pick up the e3-knight. Then going counterclockwise around the board he picks up the b2-rook, heads for the f2-pawn, and takes it, when mate in two follows. The catch is that it takes 34 moves, not 33.

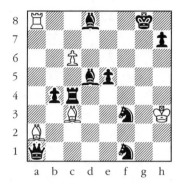

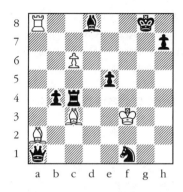

1.Kg2 2.Kf2 3.Ke2 4.Kd3 5.Kc2
6.Kb3 7.Ka4 8.Kb5 9.Ka6 10.Kb7
11.Kc8 12.Kd7 13.Kd6 14.Kxd5
15.Kd6[e6] Both here and later, (moves
37 & 39), the king may also play to e6.

27.Ke2 28.Kd3 29.Kc2 30.Kb3
31.Ka4 32.Kb5 33.Ka6 34.Kb7
35.Kc8 36.Kd7 37.Kd6[e6] 38.Kxe5
39.Kd6[e6] 40.Kd7 41.Kxd8 42.Ke7#

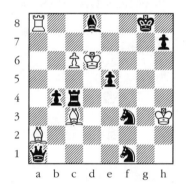

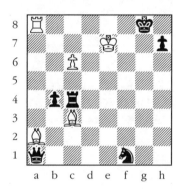

16.Kd7 17.Kc8 18.Kb7 19.Ka6
20.Kb5 21.Ka4 22.Kb3 23.Kc2
24.Kd3 25.Ke2 26.Kxf3 With the capture of the f3-knight White can finally
go after the e5-pawn.

Appendix

A few more mazes for those who can't get enough. Actually, we wanted some extras on hand in case we needed a replacement.

More Pawn Mazes

#205

1.gxh3 2.bxa7 3.bxa8=Q 4.a4 5.a5 6.a6 7.a7 8.a8=Q 9.c4 10.c5 11.c6 12.c7 13.c8=Q 14.h4 15.dxe3#

#206

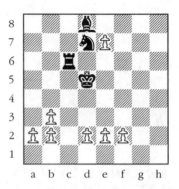

1.exd8=N 2.b4 3.b5 4.bxc6 5.cxd7 6.f4 7.f5 8.f6 9.f7 10.f8=Q 11.e3 12.d3 13.b4 14.b5 15.b6 16.b7 17.b8=Q 18.a4 19.a5 20.a6 21.a7 22.a8=Q#

#207

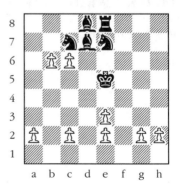

136

1.cxd7 2.b7 3.b8=Q 4.dxe8=Q
5.a4 6.a5 7.a6 8.a7 9.a8=Q 10.c4 11.c5
12.e4 13.e3 14.g4 15.g5 16.g6 17.g7
18.g8=Q 19.h4 20.h5 21.h6 22.h7
23.h8=Q#

#209

#208

1.fxe7 2.exd8=Q 3.f4 4.f5 5.f6 6.f7
7.f8=N 8.h4 9.h5 10.h6 11.h7
12.h8=Q 13.d4 14.axb4 (this could
have been played as early as move two)
15.bxc5 16.b4 17.b5 18.c6 19.c7
20.c8=Q 21.b6 22.b7 23.b8=Q 24.a5
25.a6 26.a7 27.a8=Q#

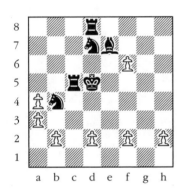

1.hxg3 2.g4 3.g5 4.g6 5.g7
6.gxh8=R[N] 7.g4 8.g5 9.e3 10.c4
11.c5 12.c6 13.c7 14.c8=Q 15.a4 16.a5
17.a6 18.a7 19.a8=Q 20.b4 21.b5
22.b6 23.b7 24.b8=Q

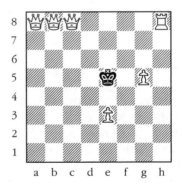

One More King Maze

#210

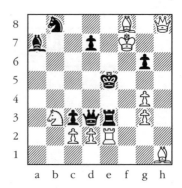

1.Kd8 2.Ke7 3.Kf7 4.Kg8 5.Kh7
6.Kh6 7.Kg5 8.Kh4 9.Kh3 10.Kh2
11.Kg1 12.Kf2 13.Ke1 14.Kd1 15.Kc1
16.Kb1 17.Ka2 18.Ka3 19.Kxb4
20.Ka3 21.Ka2 22.Kb1 23.Kc1
24.Kd1 25.Ke1 26.Kf2 27.Kg1
28.Kh2 You're halfway there.

29.Kh3 30.Kh4 31.Kg5 32.Kh6
33.Kh7 34.Kg8 35.Kf7 36.Ke7
37.Kd8 38.Kc7 39.Kxb7 40.Kc7[c8]
41.Kd8 42.Ke7 43.Kf7 44.Kg8
45.Kh7 46.Kh6 47.Kg5 48.Kh4
49.Kh3 50.Kxg2 51.Kh3 52.Kh4
53.Kg5 54.Kh6 55.Kxg7 56.Kf7#